MEMOIRS OF A WAR NURSE

SERVICE, HONOR,
&
Sacrifice

CHRISTINE R. ELMER COLLINS

— • —

DISCLAIMER

The views expressed in this book are those of the author and do not necessarily reflect the official policy or position of the Department of Defense, the United States Air Force, or the US government.
"Warning: Book contains graphic photos."

— . —

THIS BOOK, AND OUR FREEDOMS ARE DEDICATED TO

Operation Enduring Freedom

January 2009 - July 2009

ABEYTA, CHRISTOPHER PAUL
AGUILA, FRANCISCO XAVIER
BARNES, ROCCO MARTIN
BEALE, JOHN CURTIS
BENNETT, DANIEL RYAN
BESSA, JEREMY EUGENE
BLAIR, JOHN DAVID
BOWLES, TIMOTHY LOUIS
BRADSHAW, BRIAN N
BRENNAN, JULIAN THOMAS
BUNTING, BRIAN MATTHEW
BURKHOLDER, JASON EVAN
CAIN, NORMAN LEWIS III
CASILLAS, JUSTIN AARON
CASSADA, JESSIE ADAM
CHAVERS, BROCK HENRY
CHOE, FLORENCE BACONG
COLE, BRENT SCOTT
COURCY, PETER JOHN
CROSS, PETER KYLE
DAVIS, TIMOTHY PETER
DAWSON, EZRA
DE LA PENA-HERNANDEZ, ESAU IVAN
DEVOE, PATRICK ALLEN II
DEWATER, RICHARD ALLEN

DREES, STEVEN THOMAS
DUPONT, KEVIN ALLAN
ESSARY, KEITH ERIC
FAIRBAIRN, AARON ELI
FARRIS, JOSHUA RAY
FRANCESCONI, ALBERTO
GARNER, MARK ANDESS
GEARY, DANIEL JOSEPH
GIDEON, NICOLAS HUGH JOSEPH
GOODMAN, ASHTON LYNN MARIE
GRIEMEL, JARRETT PEARSON
HAGER, ROGER GARY MICHAEL
HALL, JEFFREY ALAN
HANSEN, DANIEL LOUIS
HARDT, ADAM JEFFERY
HAYES, JOHN ERIC
HERNANDEZ, JOSEPH MICHAEL
HERNANDEZ, ROBERTO ANTONIO II
HOSFORD, CHESTER WAYNE
HURT, DAVID LEE
JENRETTE, KEVIN MICHAEL
JOHNSON, ISAAC LEE JR
JOHNSON, TREVOR JERIMIAH
JONES, RICKY DEWAYNE
JORDAN, JEFFREY WILLIAM
KING, RYAN CHARLES

KULIGOWSKI, ADAM MICHAEL
LEE, CARLIE MATTISON III
LEMBKE, MATTHEW RYAN
LYNCH, TERRY JAY
MELTON, JOSHUA ALLEN
MESCALL, BRIAN MICHAEL
MISSMAN, GREGORY JAMES
MUNDEN, RAYMOND JOHN
MUNGUIARIVAS, RODRIGO AMILCA
MYERS, PHILLIP ANDREW
OBAKRAIRUR, JASPER KID
OGDEN, MATTHEW DWIGHT
OLESKI, BLAISE ADAM
O'NEILL, JONATHAN CHARLES
OUELLETTE, MICHAEL WEBSTER
PARSONS, JASON RAY
PATCH, SCHUYLER BRENT
PIRTLE, JAMES DEWEL
PREACH, KEVIN THOMAS
RAMSEY, JACOB ISRAEL
RANDOLPH, TONY MICHAEL
RATH, JOSHUA LEE
REZA, MATTHEW GREGORY
RICHARDSON, RICKY LINN JR
ROBINSON, CARLO MONTELL
ROBINSON, SIMONE ASIA

ROWE, BLUE CHARLES
ROY, MICHAEL CURRIE
SACZEK, LUKASZ DARIUSZ
SCHULTE, ROSLYN LITTMANN
SHARP, CHARLES SETH
SILVA, EDUARDO SOSA
SMALL, MARC JOSEPH
SMITH, PAUL GENE
SOUTHWORTH, JARED WILLIAM
STRATTON, MARK EDWARD II
STREAM, SCOTT BRADLEY
SUGGS, MILTON ERIC
TALBERT, CHRISTOPHER MAXWELI
TATE, DARREN ETHAN
TAYLOR, ARCHIE ANDREW
THOMPSON, DANIEL JAMES
TONER, FRANCIS LAWRENCE IV
TOWNSEND, JOSHUA RHEA
VILE, WILLIAM DAVID
WALLACE, DAVID WILLIAM III
WATSON, JASON RYAN
WEINGER, ROBERT MARTIN
WHITTLE, JOSHUA RAY
WILLIAMS, ANTHONY LEE
WILLIAMS, DERWIN ISAAC
WILSON, MATTHEW WILLARD

CONTENTS

1

— · —

PREFACE

I wrote this for Clinton, my husband.

"This," being a journal of my days in Afghanistan, or basically, the story you're about to read.

Then Clinton decided to share my journal entries with my mom, my brother, his mom, and his parents. I never asked why they started sharing, only that they did. However, those individuals started sharing the journal entries with their friends and their people.

My journals ended up all over. I'm talking not only about my hometown and family but also around the entire U.S.

It kept spiraling, almost like my words had their own energy source. They didn't stop and instead kept spreading. Readers from England, Ireland, and soon Scotland were talking about my journals. The message I was beginning to take from this viral energy was that it was more than just for Clinton.

So, I wrote more...and more...and more.

They were all about my experiences in a combat zone. Writing my stories was how I got through most days. And I always ended every entry with a focus on what I was doing, my love for my family, and, of course, my love for Clinton.

I vividly remember some feedback that I received from an English woman. She wrote back to me and said that she'd read one of my entries, which I'd titled "Rose Colored Glasses." She went into how connected she felt to my words and particularly that story, and, in a way, to my day. For a split second, I called bullshit. How could a woman in England resonate with an American woman in a war zone who is seeing death and the ugliness of humanity each and every day? How?

But in her note to me, she said that she'd had a lost day. "Shitty day", is what she actually wrote. But after reading what I had been through and how, despite the mayhem, death, and sadness I had seen, it was my ability to put on my "rose-colored glasses" and keep moving forward.

"That's what I've chosen to do today, to put on my rose-colored glasses and look at life differently," she wrote. She said it was what got her through that day.

I heard so many more stories from other readers. In fact, people were reaching back out to my mom and asking when the next entry was coming out. How funny, right? There I was in the armpit of the world, dirty, messy, and often too bloody, and people back in their own utopias were waiting with bated breath to read more.

It was then that I realized the power of sharing.

While I wrote these experiences for my husband and also hoped that perhaps my journals might help another veteran in need who'd been through the same thing I had. However, what I learned was that everyone goes through rough patches. Everyone has their own version of "shitty days." And there are so many people out there who have not served in war zones but are still fighting demons from some really dark places. In a way, they are living through a war of their own.

And that was the connection.

If you're reading this, then I feel you. And you, me. In a way, we are kindred spirits, and even though my lowest days are mine and mine alone, you need to know that you are not alone.

Not now.

Not ever.

This is for you.

2

INTRODUCTION

"There is nothing to writing. All you do is sit down at a typewriter and bleed."

- Ernest Hemingway

As soon as I arrived in "the sandbox," otherwise known as Afghanistan, I started journaling.

In fact, it was within the first 24 hours. It may sound weird, but I was very aware of my surroundings. I was very *tuned in.* And not simply "tuned in" as an American service member serving in a war zone who needs to stay "tuned in" to survive. It was a "tuning in" to everything that being there was soon to unleash and unload on me.

Reflecting on it all, I knew that I was going to Afghanistan for a purpose. I wasn't sure what exactly that purpose was, but I knew that it would be a life-changing event for me.

It all seemed to start with how I got there—the many delays in our flight, the hang-ups, all these things that played a factor in my eventual arrival and then my first patient. It was like I was meant to be there on that day, to take that first patient at that very moment. There was something profound in that event. It was more than just the patient. It was, in a way, symbolic of what the rest of my tour was going to be.

It was a deep connection in a way that I could only share by capturing it with words.

Much in the way that the Ernest Hemingway quote says. I didn't know how to write. I wasn't even sure what to write. I just knew that I had to get it out, let it out, and spill it out. I suppose the quote is true, and almost in a literal way...

I had to bleed.

In my initial journal entry, I had an epiphany. Everything clicked into place, and I understood the sequence of events that led me to that particular day. It was the day I encountered a patient whose situation required the specific work I performed. That encounter with that patient at that moment was the catalyst that inspired me to begin journaling

When I decided to start writing, my intentions were twofold.

On one hand, it was more of a catharsis—a therapy for me. Deep down inside me, there was a seed of hope that I could transfer this chaotic, traumatic, minute-by-minute experience that I knew I'd be having daily. The goal was to put it on paper to capture its essence.

On the other hand, the second part of my writing was to send home to my husband, Clinton. I wanted him to understand what that place was like and what the experience was like for me.

I wanted him to know that I was going to return a changed person and that I had written the reasons why in my journals. I wanted him to understand, later on, why. The woman, mother, wife, nurse, and American who deployed to a war zone in 2009 was not going to come home whole.

I knew I was going to be different even before I left, but I didn't know how or who I would be when I returned. My hope was that these journal entries would help Clinton better understand what I went through so that he would be somehow prepared for the woman who was (hopefully) going to come home one day.

The real truth?

The part I never shared with anyone until now in this book?

I wanted to be able to read about the woman I was, so I could read her words and find my way back if I ever got lost.

A lot of jacked-up shit happened. And I want you to know, yes you, that this is going to be a fucked-up mess.

My greatest hope now? The reason why I write this book?

Because if you're reading this, you too have likely been through, or are in the midst of, some kind of fucked up mess. Maybe this will be a beacon of light, of hope for you. Perhaps by reading my story, you'll see yourself. And in the end, you'll realize what I am still realizing today.

That the only way to truly thrive is to share it, talk about it, let it out, and live.

Fucking live!

Come on now.

Buckle up.

Lock and load.

We're going to Afghanistan.

3

MY FIRST 72 HOURS

"It's a cruel and random world, but the chaos is all so beautiful."
—— Hiromu Arakawa

Afghanistan, January 8, 2009

Amazing, absolutely amazing...the way I felt today. Over the last 72 hours, I have flown from Germany to Manas, Kirghizstan, to Afghanistan. Not only have I traveled across the world in these 72 hours, but I have done something so amazing I get emotional just thinking about it...you ask, WHAT??? What can be so amazing??? Well, I will tell you, over the past 72 hours, I have been nonstop traveling, missed flights, getting held up due to bad weather, aircraft failure, the hustle and bustle of in-processing, a change in preceptors for orientation to the unit and even a change in shift, which all lead me to one of the most important 72 hours of my life.

For the first time in my life, as a nurse, I have never felt more purposeful in what I am doing as a nurse. I took care of a young 26-year-old Romanian Coalition forces member who was fighting side-by-side with our American troops, and his mission was to be completed in just 3 days. This young guy just had his 26-year-old birthday on the 1st of January, and then on January 3rd, he ended up with blunt force trauma to the head due to an Improvised Explosive Device (IED) blast, causing a basal skull fracture. We had to evacuate an epidural bleed on the brain in order to help save his life. In addition, he also sustained an open fracture of the left hand, both eardrums were blown out, and he is on a ventilator. I was this patient's nurse...I was the lucky one to be here to help take care of him and make a difference! He was on 8 different intravenous (IV) drips, he was being artificially ventilated, and he could not speak English, so his interpreter had to be at his side 24/7 (the interpreter's name was Lt Fulga).

The patient had just been admitted a few hours before my shift began (remember the start of the 72 hours...how timing is everythin g...or maybe it was fate?). I carefully received report from the off-going nurse, and ever so meticulously, I started my head-to-toe assessment, looking at every line, every IV drip, the ventilation settings, looking at his battered and broken skull, which was held together with staples, assessing his neurological stats...as I was doing this, I noticed the patient's interpreter just watching me; he looked so sad. As I completed my assessment, I took a moment and reached out to him with a warm smile. I introduced myself and then began to ask him if he needed anything. I also began to explain to him what was going on with the patient and what the overall plan was. In addition, we went over all the IV lines, the arterial line that was placed in the patient's right wrist to help monitor his internal blood pressure; we also looked over the ventilator and cardiac monitor. I answered all the questions that he had been holding onto for the last few hours.

I could tell that Lt. Fulga was very appreciative and put at ease. He was also able to provide more accurate updates to his Commander.

I then began to focus on my patient. For the next 13 hours, I gave my all to this patient—this 26-year-old male whom I will never meet, and he will never know who Lt. Collins was. In a way, I feel as if I gave a small piece of me to him.

The last hours of my first 72.

My shift started at 0630, and there, my patient lay, ventilated, and medically sedated. Per the night shift nurse, there was no change in his status. I had gotten word from our Patient Movement Section that my patient would be air evacuated by CCATT, meaning he would be transported by a large aircraft with the Critical Care Air Transport Team. Immediately after I got to work, there was so much to do in such a short amount of time. The team would arrive in just a few short hours. As I began to get the patient ready to be transported, I made sure that I sat down with Lt Fulga. We discussed the transport, and I went over the condition of the patient (believe it or not, the patient is expected to make a full recovery).

As Lt. Fulga and I talked, I began to ask about the patient's family. My first question was, does he have a family?? And the answer to that was "YES." I then asked if the family had been notified. And that answer was also "YES."

Lt. Fulga began to tell me that the Romanian soldier has a mother and sister that he keeps in contact with. He calls the patient's family every day, and I found out that the patient's sister is also a nurse.

In no time at all, the CCATT team was here to take the soldier to Germany...talk about controlled chaos. As we packaged the patient on the transport gurney and reconnected him to the CCATT equipment, Lt. Fulga came to me and with the sincerest eyes I have ever seen in my life, he took my hand, squeezed it, and said, "Thank you, thank you so much for all you did." I simply replied, "Thank you...I was just doing my job".

He then began to say that he called his Commander and he wanted to thank me and sent his deep appreciation for the care, compassion, professionalism, and service I provided to one of their troops. I just smiled with tears in my eyes.

Lt. Fulga asked me if he could take a photo of me so that when the Romanian Soldier awoke and was recovering, he could show the soldier who took care of him and helped save his life. As they left through the trauma intensive care unit (TICU) doors, Lt. Fulga waved and smiled with a tremendous amount of gratitude radiating from his face.

It is life at its finest: living moment to moment with an uncertainty of what patient will be coming through our doors. What new challenges we may face, or what new ethical dilemma we will encounter.

During that same first 72 hours, I also had the opportunity to recover a patient from the operating room. As the patient came to our unit, something was different. This patient had a pair of blacked-out eye goggles securely over his eyes, to ensure he could not see anything, and hearing protection on so that he could not hear anything around him.

This patient was different.

This patient was an enemy combatant. He was part of the Taliban.

This particular member of the Taliban had been trying to shoot one of our helicopters down, and as a result, he ended up with a gunshot wound to the leg. The man was very fragile looking, almost malnourished; he had two Radical Islamic books with him that he had been reading prior to his hospitalization. It was strange to look into the face of a man who, if he had the chance and a weapon, would not hesitate to kill me right on the spot. As I removed the blacked-out goggles, I looked into the eyes of this man and could feel a sense of rage, horror, and hatred.

I was looking deep into the soul of an American killer.

As I helped care for this man, I could not help but think about my 26-year-old patient who was struggling to live because of something that this enemy combatant may have had a part in. As we quickly recovered this patient, we transferred him to our TICU, where he was under 24-hour watch by two fully armed guards (12G shotguns and 9mm Beretta). I still struggle thinking about caring for these people whose sole mission is to destroy and kill Americans and any others who dare try to help us. I think it will be a constant theme during my time here in Afghanistan.

4

— • —

THE FORGING

"You cannot dream yourself into a character; you must hammer and forge yourself one."
- James Anthony Froude

Miami, Arizona 1976

In the sunbaked heart of Miami, Arizona, my parents' love story unfolded. High school sweethearts who wove their futures together, like most young kids do in a small town. Initially, it seemed like a fairy tale, but like most things in life, there was no happy ending.

Our existence was etched in the rugged terrain of copper mines, where my dad labored not as an executive in a plush office but as a miner, a man who extracted wealth from the earth's veins. At one point, food stamps were our meager lifeline.

As a child, I walked this reality with innocence, blissfully unaware of our poverty until someone pointed it out. My father's arm, once whole, met its fate in a mining accident at the early age of twenty-four. The surgeons worked their miracles, reattaching it, but the aftermath lingered. He was never the same...swinging between employment and struggle, a perpetual dance on the precipice of survival.

My mom, the local seamstress, stitched our lives together. She sewed not just fabric but also hope, resilience, and the fragile threads of our family of four. In my youthful eyes, we were perfect—an amazing dad, a wonderful mom, and an older brother who alternated between protecting and tormenting me.

Yet, as I turned eight, the seams of our family began to fray.

The core disintegrated, and I witnessed the slow erosion of our once-happy existence. Shitty choices, alcohol, and other women chipped away at the foundation of my parent's marriage and our family.

The chapter of childhood innocence closed abruptly, leaving me with anger, sadness, and a gnawing sense of powerlessness.

The battleground shifted to our home. My parents' fights were raw, unkind, and relentless. Even as a young girl, I assumed the role of mediator. When my dad's voice crescendoed to my mom outside my bedroom door, I'd step between them, a tiny barrier against their storm.

One night, their argument reached a fever pitch. The walls absorbed the rage, and my heart pounded in sync with his shouts and my mom's cries. A voice, an urgent whisper, compelled me: "Go help. Help her. Go help her now!" Terrified, I threw myself into the fray. My eight-year-old frame wedged between my mom, who lay on the ground, and my dad, who towered over her,

I demanded, "DON'T HURT HER!" A desperate plea for peace.

I do not recall how I overcame that terror. But I did. I lay there, shielding my mom from the storm, absorbing the chaos into my small being. The carpeted floor cradled us, and I clung to her, my grip fierce. As I looked into the eyes of my dad, I saw something come over him; he snapped out of the trance he was in, turned around, and walked away. Everything stopped; I held onto my mom so tightly that I remember my knuckles were white as snow.

At that moment, I discovered my essence. I was a defender, a protector. More than that, I was a caregiver—an unwavering presence for those who faltered. And so, my journey unfolded: a path of standing up when others could not, of absorbing pain to shield those I loved. The terrified eight-year-old became a sentinel, forever guarding the vulnerable hearts around her.

Taking The Oath
Phoenix, Arizona 1994

When I think back to my younger self, in 8th grade, I didn't know what was next.

This may sound ass-backward, but the truth is I didn't even know HOW to go to college. I was about a year away from finishing high school, and it was never discussed as an option.

At least not for me, it wasn't.

I struggled in school—hell, I was held back in the 2nd grade. My brother Tony, in a brotherly way, never let me forget it, either. He'd tease me and tell me I was just dumb. Sure, he's my brother, but there was still a part of me that believed it. I believed what people were saying about me, even back then.

One day, I sat in my room crying, and my mom came in.

She asked what was wrong, and I told her. I shared that Tony was so smart and that everything was easy for him—sports, school, life. And me? I not only didn't know what I was good at, I had no idea what I even wanted to be. I remember desperately trying to find something that I was good at. My mom sat next to me and held my hand.

I remember my mom, as sweet as she is, holding my hand, looking at me with her little Latina face, and saying this. "Mija, you're pretty. That's what you're good at. You're good at being pretty." It seemed so stereotypical Latina mom to say that, right? Then she continued, "Because as long as you're pretty, you can get a husband. And then you can take care of your husband, have children, and keep a good home. And your husband will love you forever."

Well, that was fucking bullshit.

Looking back, that's all I can remember from that conversation that day and the fact I started crying even more. This couldn't possibly be all that life was supposed to be.

Right?

The expectation of being a female in my family was not college. It was not joining the military. It was to marry your high school sweetheart who worked in the local copper mine. He would work for 30 years and get the watch. All the while, you'd stay home, raise the children, and care for the family. All this is to say that when I graduated high school, I had no idea that you should have been looking at colleges the year before and planning out a process. I graduated in May of 1992. All my friends were like, "Hey, we're going to the valley down in Mesa to go to school at Mesa Community College."

I was frankly confused.

College? What is this? How is this?

I hadn't even applied for schools—none, zilch, zero. I had no clue how that even came to fruition. And that's when I found Pima Medical Institute, which had a program for medical assistants. Something about caring for others drew me in. At some point, the dream of being a nurse hit my radar. So, my train of thought was that this would be the closest thing I could do to nursing, and it could at least get me into healthcare. I figured I'd then meet people and figure out how to do nursing school.

I remember talking to my dad as we sat in his garage and told him I wanted to go to Pima Medical Institute. My dad said, "Had I known you wanted to go to college, I would have saved. We don't have the money, but I will help you as much as I can." They had never saved for college and couldn't afford it. I fondly remember not being upset but taking his response as a new life challenge with the overwhelming feeling of "I got this!" I felt responsible for my own future; for the first time, I felt grown-up and knew this would be the first hurdle of many I would figure out on my own. I believed in myself to get where I wanted to be. As I left the garage that day, I didn't look back.

I became more determined than ever.

I drove down to Pima Medical Institute and sat down with an admissions counselor. That lady worked out a plan with me—a plan for school, financial aid, and loans so that I could enroll and realize my dreams. Later, after graduating at the top of my class, I had a hunger for more. I really wanted to be a nurse.

That meant more school and, yes, more student loans.

Around that time, a good friend told me that the military was paying for college. I immediately thought, "No way." Skeptical at first, I soon learned it was true. In exchange for service, they would fund my college degree.

A new chapter beckoned, one I had not envisioned. My life's script, as dictated by tradition—high school, marriage, children, homemaking—was being *rewritten*. This opportunity had always been within reach; I just needed to find it.

By the summer of 1993, my parents had divorced, and I returned home, staying briefly with my dad. That fall, I spoke with a military recruiter, and in January 1994, I enlisted in the United States Air Force. Interestingly, I did not choose a healthcare role but joined the Security Forces—an Air Force Cop.

You see, there was a deep-set reason I chose to be a cop, a protector, or one who stands for others when others cannot stand. I didn't really know how deeply ingrained it was in me back then. It just seemed like the place I wanted to be at that time in my life.

My support system, aka my family, was definitely not keen on the idea of joining the military. Looking back now, it was quite humorous that my Hispanic side staged a family intervention with me. I was supposed to follow tradition, and by joining the military, they said I'd surely die.

"Be killed" is what they said.

I didn't argue with them.

In fact, I said something along the lines of "We're all going to die one day. And if God wants me to die in service to others, in the military, then that's where I need to be". They knew my mind was set because it was.

Security Forces, Peterson Air Force Base, 1994-2000

Enlisted and freshly molded by Air Force basic training and the Air Force Law Enforcement Academy mixed with Air Base Ground Defense provided by the US Army Special Forces, I found myself stationed at Peterson Air Force Base as a newly minted cop.

Curiously, my duty involved manning the C-130 flight line, counting the rivets on said C-130 aircraft, trying not to fall asleep on post, maintaining the base gate security, scrutinizing gate cards, and responding to 911 calls on base.

Timing, they say, is everything.

One evening, fate intervened. A disheveled young female airman staggered toward the main gate from the nearby dorms. Her shirt hung in tatters; she had been raped.

I scooped her up and took her to the cop shop. I made sure she was safe and never left her side until we were able to get her to a hospital for the proper medical help and treatment. I think this was maybe the first time I realized what a S.A.N.E nurse was. They are specially trained Sexual Assault Nurse Examiners, and their main job is not only to tend to the rape victims but to ensure that evidence is preserved in the event of criminal charges.

At that moment I knew exactly why I was there, at that gate, at that moment. Of all the places I could have been placed that shift, I was there for this moment alone.

Coincidence?

Nope. No such thing. I believed then, as I do now, that it was and is destiny.

'Throat Punch' Collins

US Air Force Academy, 2001

We received a call about a disturbance at the local non-commissioned officer (NCO) club. The culprits? A rowdy group of NCOs fueled by alcohol.

What a shocker... Right? I know.

My partner and I, both female Security Forces, arrived on the scene. Amidst the chaos, one NCO stood out—a behemoth of a guy. His size alone was intimidating, but I held my ground. It was time for him to leave, and I made that clear.

His response? A challenge. "What will you do if I refuse to leave?"

In that split second, my mind raced. I'm thinking, "I'll put up a fight, YES! YES! That's what I'll do, I'll put up a fight...he's big, I'll probably get my ass kicked."

So, as the NCO continued to be belligerent and confrontational in front of a large crowd of onlookers, I struck without hesitation.

A lightning-fast punch to his throat—a disabler that left him gasping, dropping to his knees. The other NCOs stared, their drunken cheers echoing. I asked them, "Who's next?"

The giant regained his breath and retreated to his dorm. That incident marked the birth of "Throat Punch" Collins. Not a badge of honor but a testament to my refusal to yield, even when fear gripped me.

From then on, whenever things got out of hand, they'd say, "Get 'Throat Punch' Collins." A lot of people don't know that nickname today. But "throat punch" Collins is still alive and well. You could probably ask my work colleagues today how much shit I take, and they'll likely say "zero" and that I stand my ground.

The challenges I faced in my youth—the doubts, the limited expectations, the lack of support—forged in me a determination to find my own path. That path led me to the Air Force, then to become an Air Force 'cop,' from there to nursing, and ultimately to that makeshift military hospital in the middle of a war.

I've seen the impact that one person can have, the ripple effect of compassion and courage. We set a powerful chain reaction in motion when we stand up for what's right and refuse to stay silent in the face of injustice.

My journey was not easy—it still isn't—but every step led me to where I needed to be—to the nurse, mother, and woman I was meant to become. But for now, we're just getting started.

I've barely shared my first 72 hours in the sandbox, and the shit hasn't even hit the fan yet.

February 1994 - Graduation from the USAF Basic Training, Lackland AFB, San Antonio, TX. A1C Christine Elmer with her parents, Clyde and Patsy Elmer

February 1994 - Graduation from the USAF Basic Training, Lackland AFB, San Antonio, TX. A1C Christine Elmer with her dad and step-mom, Clyde and Gigi Elmer

SrA Christine Elmer, 21st Security Forces Squadron, Peterson AFB, Colorado Springs, Colorado

5

— · —

A Day Just Like Any Other Day

"Being a mother is learning about strengths you didn't know you had and dealing with fears you didn't know existed."
- Linda Wooten

A fghanistan, January 9, 2009

As I sit here and think about what that phrase means to me now that I am here: "A Day Just Like Any Other Day?"

You ask, what does it mean?? Well, here in Afghanistan, today, just like any other day, has a meaning of everyday trauma, gunshot wounds, burns, suicide bombers, IED explosions, and our American troops coming to us broken and battered. I thought I had seen it all, but today..." a day just like any other day," was less than what I described above. We had a new patient; this new patient was not an American; it was not a local Afghan man; this patient was a young 14-year-old girl who had been raped by a man who her father had befriended months ago.

This man not only raped her and left dishonor to her family, but six months later, her family has now realized that she is pregnant.

This young girl's mother and brother wanted to hide the pregnancy to prevent public humiliation, so her mother took this young girl to a cowshed located behind their house, held her down while the girl's brother proceeded to cut the unborn baby from her body, using only a razor blade and string to stitch her gaping wound closed.

This poor child lay lifeless and cold in the middle of a cowshed while her brother took the newly born baby and buried it. The girl was in and out of consciousness through this horrific ordeal due to the unreal pain she felt. Remember, this is one of the poorest countries in the world; there was no pain medication, no anesthesia, there was nothing for this child.

Here with us, this sweet girl clings to life.

We are doing our best to save her; she has been on life support for the past 2 days. We continue to care for her, rid her of the lice infestation that covers her head, and diligently change her abdominal wound dressings to help with the healing process and prevent infection.

She is expected to make a full physical recovery, but the emotional wounds and scars are what I am worried about. How will those heal??? In so many other ways, I hope she doesn't make it because of what may happen at home when she returns. I am so afraid that one of their family members will kill her or sell her off as a slave. Once she is stable to move out of this hospital, I will forever wonder what has become of her. Who will take care of her when she leaves???

I sit and think about what this young girl's future holds; I still continue to pray for her and pray that she remains strong. As her father sits by her side, we will provide medical care for her and be a strong support system for her and her father.

As I began to wonder what her future holds, I heard a voice on the overhead paging system. "Level 1 Trauma," ..." Level 1 Trauma," and I immediately went to the ER to report. There were six teams waiting for wounded American soldiers. I was lucky enough to be a part of one of the six teams. We all were waiting for 6 American soldiers who were involved in a suicide bomber attack. As each trauma came through the door, I thought to myself, "This is it...this is the real war...this is the ugly face of war". In a split second, I began to wonder...if they have family, if they have children, do their mothers know they've been blown up???

This was it; my patient was here, and I began to yell out what the doctor requested, "I need 1 gram of Ancef", and "Pharmacy, I need 100 MCG of Fentanyl." as the ER doctor started his primary assessment I continued to yell out questions to the physician, "Is the trachea midline," "Do you hear bilateral breath sounds," "Equal chest expansion,"...as the dusty grayish-white floor around the gurney began to change into various shades of red, the floor transformed into a palette filled with the soldier's blood due to massive injuries, he sustained to left arm, left thigh, and right chest wall; I had to pause for a split second and take a deep breath. I had to tell myself, we will get through this; this guy is going to live, he is going to live!

As he became more stable and ready to move, we took him to the TICU, where I continued to care for him as his nurse.

As this 30-year-old Army soldier lay in our hospital bed, he began to tell me about the incident. I immediately stopped what I was doing and sat down next to him. He began to tell me that he saw the suicide bomber, he saw the vest, he should have known sooner. As he spoke, his eyes rapidly moved from right to left. His sight started to become blurry due to the collection of tears in his eyes.

I just held his hand and listened. He then told me that the suicide bomber was waiting for their Lieutenant to get closer. The bomber was trying to take out their Platoon leader. The patient saw the Taliban member push the button, and then the next thing he remembers was seeing two of his buddies dead lying close by.

I had tears in my eyes as I looked at his burnt, bloody, and dirty face.

I can't help but wonder, after all the external injuries heal, what will come of this soldier? What will happen to his emotional scars? As I sat there next to his bedside and held his hand, I was present. I was emotionally available to him; there wasn't any more exchange of words; the moment was stripped down to a nurse's ability to show compassion, understanding, and being present during one of the darkest times of this patient's life.

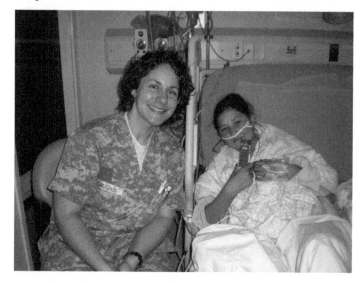

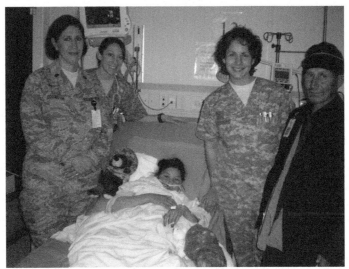

LTC Elizabeth Coddington, Capt Christine Collins, and 1st Lt Olivia Jackson

6

My First Purple Heart Ceremony

A fghanistan, January 11, 2009

The Purple Heart is awarded to any member of the Armed Forces of the United States who has been wounded or killed or who has died after being wounded in war.

The actual order of the Purple Heart includes the phrase, "Let it be known that he who wears the military order of the Purple Heart has given of his blood in the defense of his homeland and shall forever be revered by his fellow countrymen."

Today was my first Purple Heart Ceremony. We had two American soldiers on life support. One of them had bilateral tibia and fibula fractures; he had pins, screws, and rods coming out from all angles of both his lower extremities; we couldn't keep enough padding on the bed to soak up all the blood that was oozing from both legs. We even had to put padding on the floor to catch the blood as it dripped from the sides of the bed. Both soldiers were medically sedated. As rows of people gathered around their bedsides, a US Army General was there to speak on behalf of these two soldiers and present their Purple Hearts...as a Private called "Attention to Orders," everyone stood at attention. I took a big sigh and scanned the room. I looked at both men who were lying there lifeless, and I thought to myself, "Sadly, this will not be my last Purple Heart ceremony." As all the Army and Air Force troops paid their respects to these heroes, we quickly packaged the patients to fly out to Germany.

I can't help but wonder about their mothers, their sisters, and their grandmothers...are they worried? Are they scared? I hope they know that we are taking good care of them and we are doing everything in our power to help them LIVE, including lots and lots of prayer.

It's amazing, over the past three days, I have had the opportunity to take care of our soldiers...initially there were six American troops that were on foot patrol, and a suicide bomber attacked them. One of our patients was lucky and only escaped with minor injuries. However, his good friend, in the same blast, lost his arm and potentially his leg. The same platoon lost two of their really good men. As my patient began to run through the sequence of events that happened on the 8th of January, I could see him reliving each second of that one moment...that one moment that completely changed his life forever and the lives of many others.

I just ask myself, "Why?"

After responding to the ER for another mass trauma on the 9th of January, we had two more American troops injured in an IED explosion...I don't think all of this has hit me yet. I just go and do what I am trained to do...I can't think about it. When I catch myself thinking about everything, I find myself thinking of my own children and begin to cry. I think as I sleep, my brain tries to make sense of what has happened during the day and begins to process images that I have seen throughout the day...makes complete sense of why I had my first nightmare last night. What I can recall from the nightmare is that I was located on an airfield, and we (the Americans) were being overrun by the Taliban, and as I continued to fight, a man wearing all white garb blew my right arm off. The same man began to fire rounds at me as I ran for cover.

I can still vividly remember thinking to myself as I was running, "Okay, my arm is blown off, that's okay, I am still alive, I can make it." What is sad for me is that I know this will be the first of many but as I continue to journal, I firmly believe that this will help me through tougher times that are to come once the weather gets warmer. My only hope is that I can continue to cope with all my experiences, here in this war zone, in a healthy and positive way so that I can be of good service to my country and to my family when (if) I make it home.

I continue to struggle with being separated from my husband and children. My biggest fear is that something will happen to my girls, and I will not be there to hold them while they are crying (just like I am sure all the mothers of the boys that I have been caring for).

There is so much guilt I feel inside as a mother of three daughters. If I think about it too long, my eyes begin to fill with tears.

I received an email from my husband today that stated Taylor, my middle daughter, who is 4 years old, slipped while getting out of the bathtub and needed medical attention. She ended up needing staples on the back of her head to close a laceration. I only wished I could have been there to love her and tell her that everything was going to be alright.

I am her mother, and that's what we do as moms...or at least we should do. I can only imagine what my husband went through...especially the thought of having to tell me (I have to giggle on that one).

Afghanistan is going to be one fucked up and crazy ride. Kandahar and Kabul are so volatile right now, and as the weather gets warmer, the Taliban will be emerging from their hidden, dark, and dreary caves, ready to fight...we will have even more mass casualties on a daily basis.

When I read about Kandahar and Kabul in the paper and news, it's hard to believe that I am so close to these hot zones.

As I wake up each morning feeling beaten, soar, and tired, I do a countdown...only 172 more days; then I think to myself, "Can I really do this? Can I really keep this up??" It is non-stop...I have to remind myself; I don't have a choice, I am here and I WILL DO THIS, I WILL get through this and leave with the same sparkle in my eyes that I came with.

I will continue to persevere.

7

— • —

MOTHER HEN

"I hadn't thrown a punch in years, but for her, I'd fight the world."
—— Kristen Callihan, Make It Sweet

Afghanistan, January 13, 2009

When I hear the phrase "Mother Hen," I can picture an exceptionally large white hen with four or five chicks behind her. She is willing to do just about anything to protect her babies.

Or better yet, I can picture a very large woman who is really pissed off and willing to "throat punch" anyone who is trying to hurt or get at her children. There is always something about when a person is punched in the throat who is acting inappropriately. Somehow, things get noticeably clear. Not sure if it's because they have a temporary loss of airway that things make sense and become clear.

But anyway, today, I was that mother hen and l was that force to be reckoned with. I was the protector of our sweet 14-year-old female patient. For those who truly know me you know what kind of ugly picture is about to unfold, especially when I start the conversation with my right brow slightly curled upward and in a low-key voice, "I am a little confused?"

This patient's assigned nurse came to me to show me a business card of a lady who was visiting on behalf of a women's organization here in Afghanistan. As I looked over to where this lady was sitting, I watched her briefly as she began to talk to the patient's father; I could see the distress on his face. I just felt that something wasn't right. As I spoke to the interpreter, she informed me that this lady wanted to interview our 14-year-old patient and take a picture of her to show the public she was still alive.

Yeah, I don't think so.

I quickly walked to where this lady sat and introduced myself. It became noticeably clear to me that someone else had sent her to our hospital to investigate the situation and get more information from inside the hospital. For the safety of the patient and the protection of the family, I immediately restricted access to the patient and retrieved our commanding officer, LTC Elizabeth Coddington, while removing the woman from the TICU.

Apparently, the story of our 14-year-old patient is big news here in Afghanistan. It is all over the news, and there are some people who want her to live and others who want her dead. We have interpreters here within the hospital which helps us communicate with our patients. It has become clear that one of them has been leaking information to the local press; the stories that are being reported are grossly misinterpreted, and we are not sure who to trust. There are only a few of the locals who are considered trusted agents, and we will continue to trust these agents until the child is safe.

The child's father is in complete distress. He has no money; he and his son were the only two that were working on a farm in the mountains of Afghanistan to provide food for the family on a daily basis. The family is being cast out of their village. People are throwing rocks and ridiculing them for what has happened.

The son is in prison, and according to Afghan law, it is the family's responsibility to provide food and water during his imprisonment. However, because the father is here, no one is able to bring food or water to his son. He is completely tormented by the situation. I can see he is suffering from a broken heart. When I look into his eyes, I can see the hurt and anger in his eyes. He's falling apart piece by piece. I feel so helpless it is difficult to sit and watch someone suffer every day, and there's nothing I can do or give him to make it better.

According to the father, their lives are in jeopardy.

Everyone has turned their backs on them. What is sad is to see the father having to make a choice to either stay here with his daughter or go back home to check on his son and family to see if they are still alive.

This place is incredibly frustrating at times. I fear for the family but mostly for the child. There are so many people who want to see this child dead; however, we, the nurses, have all bonded together to keep her with us as long as we can. We will keep her safe; we will help her heal, we will love and protect her, and she will be safe with us. I only wish that I could adopt her and bring her home with me.

During one of my talks with an interpreter, she began to tell me how lucky I was to be born in the United States. Anywhere but here in Afghanistan, the interpreter said, "This girl would not be suffering from this pain, this trauma, and ridicule." She's right. No woman or child should have to suffer from this type of situation. I just wish there were more I could do for her. When she leaves us, I'll forever wonder what happened to her and her father.

I thank God every day for being born in the United States and for all that I have. I am so incredibly rich, not in the monetary sense but in the sense of family. My husband loves me unconditionally, and I have three beautiful, healthy daughters who are all just as tenacious as their mother.

I am sure playing Mother Hen has not given me much popularity or lifelong friends, but fuck-it, what I know is the fragile, scared, hurting man who sits diligently by his daughter's bedside knows that I care and I will protect her at all costs.

8

— · —

AN AMERICAN DEATH

"A hospital alone shows what war is."
- Erich Maria Remarque, All Quiet on the Western Front

Afghanistan, January 17, 2009

CNN headlines read," Suicide bomber kills seven in Kabul. "...and the officer in charge of the ER is running to the TICU, stating we have potentially six fresh traumas coming our way!

We gathered all the TICU staff and put a plan together. We split half of our staff to respond to the ER when the traumas arrived, and the other half was busy preparing the TICU for our newly wounded American soldiers.

The first Soldier rolled in on life support.

She was a young female Army soldier who was severely burned over 50% of her body. As we began to stabilize her in the ICU, the next trauma came rolling in. A large, 34-year-old male who had pictures of his young children tattooed on his right forearm.

No sooner than he comes into our unit, we begin to code him.

The code leader quickly assigned everyone their roles, and I became the medication nurse. I was at the head of the bed with the surgeon and the rest of our team members. We first started with epinephrine through the soldier's central line, which was placed in his neck. We did round and round of epinephrine every 3-5 minutes while we continued to do chest compressions.

The surgeon at the bedside decided to do an open thoracotomy.

This is when the physician cuts open the left chest wall and uses his own hand to pump the heart. This soldier was dying right before my eyes. There was blood everywhere, flowing from the bed, drenching the floor and our shoes. As I continued to push drugs via his central line, I could see his entire unit peering into the windows through the corner of my eyes.

They were all trying to get a sign or a glimpse of this soldier to reassure them he was still alive. As we continued to work on this 34-year-old young man, we began to rapidly infuse over 16 units of packed red blood cells and fresh frozen plasma, including lactated ringers. We hoped that the volume resuscitation that we were giving would be enough to help pump his heart. As the doctor continued to use his hand to pump this soldier's heart, we were FINALLY able to get a shockable rhythm. Everyone stood by as we placed the internal paddles inside the chest wall, cradling the heart from side to side.

The doctor yelled, "I am clear, you're clear, everyone's clear."

The patient was shocked. We got a heartbeat back, but it wasn't for long. We continued to push fluids and drugs to help the heart continue to beat, but it just wasn't enough. We could not do enough for him. We coded this soldier for what seemed to be a lifetime; no one wanted to give up. We all took turns doing chest compressions, and we all wanted him to live.

As a doctor finally called the code, we all reluctantly stopped.

As one of the surgeons began to close the open chest wall, which exposed the patient's heart, he began to cry. I had tears in my eyes. I tried to look around, but everything was blurry. I had to stay focused. I couldn't cry, not in front of everyone. I quickly regained my composure and began to clean the patient. We washed his burnt, bloody skin and made him presentable for the members of his unit to say their last goodbyes. It was so painful to see each member who stood next to him over the last several months say goodbye to him. I was so overrun with emotions but remained steadfast. I was there to help his unit. I let members cry on my shoulder, and all I could offer them was a hug and a simple statement: "I'm so sorry for your loss."

They knew we did everything we could for him. We worked so hard to save his life, but it just wasn't enough. It was his time to go.

What is amazing to me is when I take a moment to think about this morning's events, way before the explosion, I'm talking about the early morning when this man woke up and got ready for the day; *he had no idea this was the day he was going to die.*

He had no idea that the particular road he was traveling on would be the exact road where a suicide bomber would be waiting for him. Interestingly enough, the suicide bomber chose a location close to a large fuel truck. When he detonated the bomb, the blast was so great that it carried our young female patient out of her seat in the Humvee and pinned her between the vehicle and concrete barrier, where she continued to burn alive. As for our 34-year-old soldier, the explosion blew him out of the Humvee up into the air, landing on top of a large cement barrier where no one knew where he was until the Dust-off team flew in and saw him lying on top of the barrier.

I'm so tired today that I could barely drag my feet home. HOME. What a far-off and distant dream to me.

I miss home.

I love home.

I can't wait to go home

Sgt Carlo M. Robinson, 2008-2009 Afghanistan

9

— • —

A DAY FOR REFLECTION

"Life can only be understood backwards; but it must be lived forwards."

—— **Søren Kierkegaard**

Afghanistan, January 19, 2009

Today was a great day to reflect on all the things we have accomplished collectively as a critical care unit.

We started on this journey only 19 days ago, but there has been so much that has happened, too much to digest in the brief time that has passed. I am fully aware of my surroundings and those who surround me.

I can feel the mistrust of the local Nationals and the translators that we work side by side with. I can feel the uncertainty of newer nurses, Physicians, and technicians as they start their path in the TICU. At times it is too much to deal with and to comprehend.

So, this brings us to today.

Can you believe that we only have one patient in our TICU, and the patient is pretty much on autopilot. We are just waiting to transfer the local national to a new facility. Needless to say, we all had a lot of time today, which is good for a change.

It was such a great feeling to know there was not someone dying in the bed next to me or someone with their limbs blown off. I actually had time to go to my room and *just be*. Wow, to just be and sit alone with no noise, no loud alarms from cardiac monitors, no one screaming, no one dying. It was a day of reflection for me, a day that I needed so desperately.

As I sat in my dark, quiet room, I began to cry as I thought about the 34-year-old man who lost his life two nights ago. I kept going over and over the events that played out that night, thinking of everything we did and what we could have done differently.

Each time, I had the same ending. He died, and there was nothing we could do about it.

I guess the hardest part for me was the fact that he had children. I'm sure at the start of his deployment, he kissed his children goodbye and told each of them that he loved them more than anything in this world and that he would think of them every second of every day, promising he would come home to love and hug them again. I think of that promise he made to his family, to his children, to his mother, and to his wife. He reminds me of my own goodbye to my children and my husband, saying the same words that I'm sure echoed throughout his home. Then I think, what makes me so different?

At least now I know his name. When they come to us from the battlefield, it's not like they have a driver's license and insurance card handy. Usually, they come blown up

His name is Carlo. Sergeant Carlo M. Robinson. He is a father of two from Hope, Arkansas. I know I'll never forget each and every single detail of his passing. This one will be etched in the depths of my soul for all my natural born days.

When tragedy hits, we always say, "Why me, why me." With everything that I have seen and experienced in such a brief time in Afghanistan, I now think, ***"Why not me? Why not me?"***

I know that when I leave this place I will forever be changed. I will no longer be the same Christine I once was. War is ugly. War changes everything. I can't say at this point and time, how I will be different or what specifically will be different about me; I just know I will be.

I continue to thank God for the gift he has given me: a loving, understanding, and enduring husband who stands by me without the slightest waiver.

My husband is an astonishing man who has always loved me unconditionally. I thank him now for what he must do while I'm gone and what he'll have to be once I return home. His inner soul is so beautiful, and his patience is endless. He handles me with such care and respect he knows just what to say at just the right moment. He is my hero! I'm so thankful that he is home waiting for me, loving me and supporting me through this life-changing event and loving her three daughters enough for the both of us. I continue to thank him for telling my beautiful girls that I love them every night as they go to bed and that mommy thinks of them every second of every day. And most importantly that mommy will be coming home.

Clinton is a remarkable person, magnificent dad, and all the sacrifices that he makes daily for our family. Even those sacrifices he does not share with anyone else and keeps to himself. He is truly one of a kind, and I am so proud to be called his wife.

Today...well today was a day for reflection of what has come, what is now, and what is to come.

10

---·---

MR. MOM

"Of all the titles I've been privileged to have, Dad has always been the best."

-Ken Norton

Afghanistan, January 19, 2009

Clinton.

He was the rock, the foundation, and home.

During my deployment, my colleagues started hating me. Of course, I say that tongue in cheek. It was because that guy religiously sent me one to two boxes a week. Every FUCKING week that I was deployed. Mail call was the fun part of the day... when the NCOIC called out their name, and "COLLINS!" was yelled, everyone rolled their eyes, and laughter broke out. Of course, I walked up to the front as if I were walking down a runway, with my head held high while collecting my treasures from across the world.

Clinton sent me care package, after care package, after care packages. He never failed, never faltered. Whatever I needed, he sent to me. And even if I didn't ask for anything, he still sent me stuff. He would send me stuff for the children. He would have the girls go through their old toys and send me Barbie, stuffed animals, and posters.

Clinton was that rock. He was the foundation. He was there, so I didn't have to think about what was happening at home. He took care of everything back home.

I was so proud of Clinton, and even more proud as he was featured on "The Early Show" on CBS News. The topic of the show was:

"Military "Mr. Moms" Wage War At Home. While Wives Are Deployed, Husbands Are Taking On The Role Of Stay-At-Home Dads."

That was literally the name of the segment, and he, as well as my three daughters, were featured on the show. Clinton had been in the Air Force before, so he really understood the commitment it takes not only to serve but also to deploy—and even more so, to deploy to a war zone. I think that was what made things smoother for us. I won't say easy because separation never is, but smoother is what comes to mind.

The segment also went on to say:

"While his wife, Christine, is deployed in Afghanistan as an Air Force Captain and trauma nurse, Clinton lives on base, raising their three daughters – Kennedy, 12, Taylor 4, and Reagan, 2...The Collins children talk to their mother via Skype and are getting used to dad's style of cooking, cleaning, and doing their hair."

Was I one of the lucky ones?

I don't know.

All I know is my story at that place and time. But knowing my story and all that transpired, I can say from my vantage point that, yeah, I was one of the lucky ones. I missed the hell out of him and my girls. But I knew that they were in the best hands possible.

It's a strange comparison, the chaos and trauma of war set against the steadfast love of family. But perhaps that is the very essence of the human experience – finding those moments of grace and connection amidst the struggles we all face.

For my little 14-year-old female patient, her struggle was one no child should ever have to endure. The physical and emotional scars of her injuries were compounded by the absence of her mother's comfort. For me, it was the daily battle to keep going and caring, even as my heart ached for my own daughters half a world away.

The Collins Girls while Christine was deployed. Kennedy 11 yrs, Taylor 4 years, Reagan 16 months old

11

— · —

A Day Without War

"War does not determine who is right - only who is left"
- Bertrand Russell

A fghanistan, January 20, 2009

A day without war would be a day without wounded innocent children in this country.

Today, we received a 3-year-old Afghan child flown in from a forward operating base. She came to us on life support with a depressed skull fracture due to shrapnel that protruded out the left side of her skull. In addition, she suffered from internal bruising, which required an abdominal exploratory lap and additional surgical intervention to repair her left hip due to a puncture wound received from shrapnel penetrating to the bone.

As you begin to wonder, "What in the world happened? ".."How could this have happened?"...."why did this happen?" well, this day, this morning, a suicide bomber was on a mission. His mission was to ram the front gate of one of our forward operating bases, and this suicide bomber was prepared. He was so prepared that he had enough explosives to send shockwaves felt miles away. This suicide bomber was able to ram the first of two gates with a large vehicle strapped with over 1500 lbs. of homemade explosives. At the second gate, the base police were able to fire multiple rounds of ammunition through the driver's window, which killed him. Sadly, prior to his death, he managed to set the bomb off, killing and wounding many innocent people in the surrounding area.

The shrapnel flew so fast and so chaotically that no one was safe. Not even this 3-year-old child. When she came to us, she was alone; there was no one by her side, and her parents were nowhere to be found. Everyone was wondering to whom this sweet child belonged. As the hours passed, the child was ready to be extubated. She had been back from the operating room (OR), from which she received an emergency craniotomy and additional surgical interventions. As she began to wake up, she opened her large brown eyes, and everyone could tell she was terrified.

She just began to cry and call out for her mother.

Even though she was in pain, I immediately scooped her up in my arms and just held her ever so tight. I began to sing to her. I began to sing her songs that I would sing to my own three daughters. She just looked at me with these amazing brown eyes as tears streamed down her face. We had already given her IV morphine, and there was not much else we could give her. I just loved her and rocked her until she fell fast asleep. It took over 4 hours, but she was asleep and felt safe. As the day passed, we found out that her mother, who was 4 months pregnant, was also injured in the attack.

The mother had been hospitalized at a different hospital miles and miles away. She received severe injuries to her back and her left shoulder. We also discovered that her father had died from a suicide bomber just a few months prior.

As I rock the sweet child, I began to think about this war and what it is doing not only to the people of Afghanistan but to our own people.

Our own men and women from the United States of America. All of this...for what?

As we continue to fight the Taliban and we continue to lose more precious men, women, and children, I hope that all of this will be worth the trophy at the end of the day. I dreamed that in the future, there will be a republic of Afghanistan where women are free to vote, to have a voice, to be educated, and to have a choice. To know what it is like to live free!

Thirty to forty years from now, when I'm rocking my own grand-children to sleep, I hope I can look back and know that what I have done has made a lasting contribution to the overall good of this country. The men and women who have paid the ultimate sacrifice will not be in vain but in good faith that this country will thrive and prosper. That the people of the Republic of Afghanistan will know of war, but only in the past, and will cherish their newfound freedom which so many Americans take for granted daily.

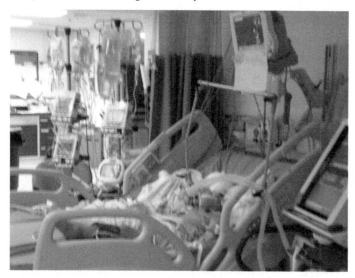

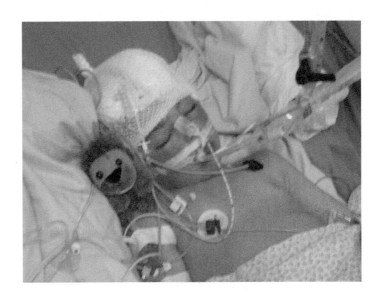

12

—·—

SAYING GOODBYE

**"Goodbye may seem forever. Farewell is like the end, but in my
heart is the memory and there you will always be."**
— Walt Disney

Afghanistan, January 24, 2009

As today began to wind down from a busy day in the TICU
with multiple traumas from an IED blast, getting the American patients ready to fly to Germany via the Critical Care Air Transport
Team. Then, dealing with three enemy combatants who had been
injured two days prior, they were the sole survivors of a 23-member
Taliban unit. We extubated one of the three today.

One of the three enemy combatants had been extubated (taken
off life support, as he was doing well and improving). This enemy
combatant quickly woke up from his medically induced coma and
began swinging to strike my technician and me, then he proceeded to
spit in our faces...even after his fucked up behavior, we continued to
care for him, ensuring he was comfortable and all his medical needs
were taken care of...can you believe the patient even bit one of our
technicians; can you say "Throat Punch!"

Not that I did, but I sure wanted to.

These events were definitely tiresome periods, but I must say the most important and time-stopping moment was when I had to sit down with my sweet 14-year-old patient, who, three weeks ago, had a traumatic c-section performed by her brother. Somehow, someway, I had to search deep in my heart to find the right words to explain that she would be transferring to a new hospital outside the walls of our protection within the next day or two.

How do you find the words? What is it that you say? What can you say to make this child feel safe...when all she has known is me and two other nurses caring for her every need, safeguarding her safety, and loving her as if she were our own child? What would I say?

I began to look for a female interpreter. Of course, there was not one to be found except for a wonderful and soft-spoken gentleman who was willing to help. I respectfully asked the father's permission to have a male interpreter assist us in our conversation. The great thing was that the father had built a trusting relationship with this particular interpreter; therefore, the father was more than happy to have him help. Before we walked into the patient's room, I pulled the interpreter aside and told him, "No matter what I say to her, please translate all my words and phrases in the most loving and kind way humanly possible"; "I have to know that she truly knows that we love and care about her and we truly care what happens to her, You understand, right?!" The interpreter nodded and smiled, and I knew just by what I saw in his eyes I felt he was being honest with me. I felt comfortable and confident that he was the right person to help me.

As I took a deep breath and passed the threshold of her door, I knew from the pit of my stomach that this would be difficult and that this was one of those moments in my life that I will remember forever. As I entered the young 14-year-olds room with her father and the interpreter, her eyes locked onto me, her face lit up as bright as the sun on a hot summer's day. I just smiled back and sat down next to her while she reached out for my hand. With the help of the interpreter, I began to tell her how proud I was of her; she had gotten so strong and that she had done an amazing job in getting better.

As I continued to talk, she began to gleam full of delight and accomplishment. I then began to tell her how much she means to us and that we will always be here for her ...she squeezed my hand, and I began to smile. She said to me, "Hooba," "Hooba," which means "good - good." I began to shake my head up and down, saying, "Yes, yes...good, good, you did a good job...you did it...I am so proud of you!"

In an instant my eyes looked down at the sheets of her bed because my eyes began to fill with tears, I could barely get a word out...I had to stop, I just couldn't get any more words out, the room was so quiet, you could hear a pin drop. As I looked up at the once smile that covered this young girls face...that gleaming smile was slowly slipping away...she now had a look of confusion and was unsure of what was coming next.

I tightly grabbed her hand and smiled...I told her, "You are doing such an amazing job and getting better that it is time for you to go...you are going to go to a better hospital where you will continue to get stronger and heal completely". As those words passed my lips and moved through the interpreter's words, my sweet 14-year-old patient began to cry...it was almost as if I felt like my own child was hurt, and all I wanted to do was take away the pain...I felt a hole in my heart...a hole that I knew I couldn't fill. As I began to try and smile with tears streaming down my face, I looked around the room and noticed that everyone was crying.

The father began to say that he owes everything to us, that we brought his daughter back from the dead. We all hugged each other, as in some way this would make it all better...well, it didn't, it didn't work; this time, a hug just wasn't enough.

Thoughts were racing through my mind a million miles a minute...if there was any way to keep her here with us, surely I would be able to find a way. Well, this time, I came out empty-handed. This poor girl had been through so much...first, she was raped, then ended up pregnant, and her mother and brother proceeded to cut the life out of her body in such a way that is unforgiving...after two days of bleeding and her condition worsening, her father realized that his daughter was truly sick, and the truth was then revealed...this is when he made the decision to save his daughter's life. The father grabbed his lifeless daughter and placed her on the back of a donkey, which she rode for 2 days in the mountains of Afghanistan until they reached a truck where they were able to get a ride into Kabul. After being hospitalized in Kabul for a few days, it was arranged for her to come to Bagram.

We all immediately fell in love with her; we all gave her everything we had:...around the clock care, around-the-clock dressing changes, multiple treatments of RID to exterminate the lice that covered her hair..., and we brought her back to a healthy state. We all worked non-stop for her...we all were willing to do whatever it took to get her better...and she did! She did get better...we all are so proud, and now it is time to say Good-bye... goodbye to our sweet child. I must say that we all are worried; we hope and pray that she remains safe.

I will forever remember this day; this was a day that I broke some-one's heart... the heart of a child. I will truly cherish my special mo-ments with her...taking her outside for the first time so that she can feel the cool crisp breeze on her face, catching snowflakes in her hands and watching them melt. Seeing her facial expression as she felt the raindrops fall on her face, finding out that she did not like the feeling at all; in fact, she squinted her nose and eyes and ran back inside while I stayed in the rain dancing and laughing.

I will forever remember her looking at the mountain range that surrounds our base and her pointing in the sky, telling me that she flew in the air to get here. My most favorite moment with her was when we would dance down the halls of the hospital together...at first, she thought I was crazy, but that only lasted two seconds. As I began to dance to my own beat, she started to laugh so hard she could barely stand up.

Lt. Olivia Jackson was by my side doing the running man...then Dr. Wink walked around the corner at just the right time and busted out into laughter but joined the fun, too...before we knew it, we had an audience, and everyone began to dance.

You should have seen the look on this child's face...it stopped time.

That moment was priceless and sacred. She had never seen anything like this before; she continued to laugh all the way back to the TICU. This was one of those moments that I will remember and will make me smile as my journey continues here; I can only pray that she will remember each bright moment amidst her tragedy and continue to smile thinking of us, knowing that we loved her, her forever family. We will miss her so much...this was my goodbye, my goodbye to our little Angel.

The very best...1st Lt Olivia Jackson, Trauma/ICU Nurse. One hell of a nurse and combat sister

13

— . —

THE TALIBAN

"Just that you do the right thing. The rest doesn't matter. Cold or warm. Tired or well-rested. Despised or honored"
- Marcus Aurelius

A fghanistan, January 29, 2009

How is it that we do what we do?

Today, for 14 hours, I dealt with nothing but enemy combatants. That is all we had in our TICU. My patient was extremely ill. He has a bolt placed in his head to measure his intracranial pressures (ICP). Due to the fact that this patient is not doing well and has suffered a traumatic brain injury (TBI), the ICP has to be monitored every hour, with clamping and unclamping the ventriculostomy to measure how much fluid is coming off the brain. We need to ensure his ICP does not go above a set level due to the pressure in the brain. Needless to say, he is on life-support, and his vital signs are at times unstable.

It is frustrating for me because just last week, this was the same man who spit on me and tried to punch us and bit one of our technicians, and still here I am, diligently caring for him as if he were my brother. I am giving my all; I cannot leave his bedside. I am on my feet for the whole 13–14-hour shift. Just to ensure he does not die.

For what?

Why?

This is what I ask myself repeatedly. I look at him, and it is hard not to see his mother or even maybe a child he might have. Who the hell knows? I just know that we are doing our best to help him recover from this traumatic brain injury he sustained while trying to kill OUR American soldiers. As I continue to care for this man, who looks so much like a boy, we get a new admission from the Emergency Room. He's another member of the Taliban who is a prisoner at our base prison. He came to us in septic shock and was also placed on life support. As his nurse got him settled, she then stepped away for just a moment to get a specific drip he needed for his blood pressure. As soon as she stepped away, the patient's ventilator started alarming; I noticed that the man was biting his ET tube, and he was fighting the vent. I quickly went to the patient's bedside and noticed that his blood pressure was 30/20's; a normal blood pressure is usually around 110 to 130 systolic.

My good friend Olivia was at my side, I yelled for the patient's nurse, and I quickly disconnected the ventilator and began to bag him with a bag-valve-mask bag (BVM). At the same time, I yelled, "Get the code cart." Before I knew it, chest compressions were being done by Olivia; I quickly opened up the code card and began pulling drugs.

We worked on this Taliban member for another five minutes. It seemed like much longer, though. Not only did we continue CPR, but the surgeon had to place a chest tube in this man.

During all of this, we had another Taliban member who was lying in the adjacent bed from where we were working on the prisoner/patient. This patient is recovering from burns covering the right side of his head and upper body from a rocket-propelled grenade (RPG) that blew up in his face as he was trying to bomb US soldiers. This enemy combatant continues to curse at us and harshly threatens he is going to kill us. It is so frustrating for me to do this at times.

We have Army guards who are given specific orders to secure patients who are enemy combatants and the new prisoner admission. The looks on their faces, due to the constant care and life-saving interventions we are giving to the enemy, are glaringly evident. The looks on their faces say it all. I could hear one of the guards say in disgust, "Why are they saving him? They should just let him die."

After the code was done and the prisoner became stable, a couple of the guards wouldn't even look or talk to us. I am sure that this is hard for them to understand why we continue to care for the Taliban even after all the pain and misery they do to our US and Coalition forces. It is hard for us as healthcare professionals to do what we do, especially in a war zone.

I don't ever expect anyone to understand what I do or what I have to do with all this.

All I know is that I'm going to do the right thing. No matter how much I continue to have my inner struggle of caring for these enemy combatants, there is such a fine line between doing what is right and the latter.

I will continue to remain focused and do what I know is right, no matter how much I get spat on, punched, bitten, or even threatened that I will be killed.

14

— · —

ANGRY AND FRUSTRATED

**"I can be changed by what happens to me, but I refuse to be
reduced by it."**

– Maya Angelou

A fghanistan, February 2, 2009

Today, I just felt so incredibly angry and frustrated in so
many ways.

There are several reasons for this. We still have our two enemy combatant patients, including one prisoner who almost died a couple of
days ago. We coded him twice, and he came back. Due to our nursing
shortage, we are now working 5 days straight, 13–14-hour shifts with
one day "on call," and we have ONE scheduled day off during the
month of February.

Sigh...

I cannot say how important my 1-day off during my work week is.
I truly need this time to be able to decompress and get my mental state
back to "normal", whatever normal means. This week has been not
only emotionally draining but physically as well.

I have been caring for both enemy combatants since last week, and
they both are getting better, which is surprising to the physicians.

Most of their IV lines and fluids have been discontinued, and they don't need to be "medically" monitored as closely as they once were.

However, they both need to be supervised very closely due to the fact that they are disgruntled and combative. Today, I was the primary nurse for an enemy combatant with a traumatic brain injury. It's interesting to watch both of these patients because they pretend not to understand or speak English. They even act as if they can't move their bodies.

There are armed guards that sit inside our open bay as we care for these men to ensure everyone's safety.

You see, my patient ended up having a stroke during his operation at the end of January, and it was assumed that he had lost much of his movement on the right side of his body...he is weak and unable to feed or walk on his own. He is a "total care" patient. Or at least he acts like he is.

Most of these enemy combatants speak English and can do for themselves, but they know if they act like they are sick and purposefully do not respond when we ask questions, they then stay at our hospital until they get better or until they can transfer to a confinement facility with health care that will meet their needs, instead of being transferred directly to the local base prison.

There is so much time and energy spent caring for my patient who is thin and resembles a teenage boy. I must do everything for him. Feed him, give him a bath, wipe the drool from his face, and wipe his backside too.

This leads me to the number one reason I'm so frustrated.

As I was getting my supplies ready to give this patient a shot of insulin at the bedside, I turned my back to him to pick up an alcohol wipe that I placed at the edge of the bed. And as I turned my back, out of nowhere and with all this man's strength, he proceeded to punch me in the lower back over my kidney.

As he punched me, I spun around and realized that he had both of his feet up in the air and was ready to kick me in the face. Needless to say, mother fucker, it was on! I looked at him right in his eyes and said, "you fucked with the wrong person today."

I grabbed him by his throat with one hand and then grabbed his knees with my other hand and placed him back down on the bed very firmly. It happened so fast, and before I knew it, there were two armed guards by my side and two other nurses who were there holding his legs. We ended up putting him in four-point restraints to not only protect him from himself but to protect us as well. It did not end there.

He then decided that he would continue to try and spit at us, and then he began to poop in the bed. We cleaned up his poop almost every two hours until our shift ended. His buddy lying across the bay decided to start the same shenanigans. I was annoyed and frustrated that once we got my patient cleaned up, then the other enemy combat would start shitting. It would take us up to an hour to clean one patient. Changing the sheets, removing equipment, placing the equipment on the patient, then repositioning the patient and placing cream on the patient's skin to help prevent skin breakdown.

Enough was enough!

I had to walk away for a moment just to get my head right. I decided not to show how frustrated I was, especially to these two assholes, because I knew they would enjoy seeing me upset. To them, it would be a weakness on my part. So, I just smiled and laughed with my girl Olivia as each patient decided to take turns shitting.

This job can get so incredibly frustrating at times because we are caring for these enemy combatants, all the while we know for 100%

that they were trying to kill our American soldiers and coalition members. It's so hard at times. I must remind myself of the mission and why I've been placed here.

That I am here to make a difference.

I am here to help.

I am here to help win the minds and hearts of the Afghan people.

If that is what I have been doing for the past couple of weeks with these enemy combatants, then this is what I must do.

It is not easy by any means, and it continuously wears on my heart and mind. But it is something that must be done.

I can do this, and I will do this.

I will be a better person because of this incredible experience.

In some strange way, I think if I continue to tell myself this, I'll believe it and be that better person in the future.

15

— · —

KARMA

"As she has planted, so does she harvest; such is the field of
karma."
— **Sri Guru Granth Sahib**

Afghanistan, February 9, 2009

Today, one of my patients was a 6-month-old baby who
weighed just under 10 pounds ...YES, a 6-month-old baby that
weighed less than 10 lbs. This little baby looked like a newborn. This
little guy had a cleft palate and needed a repair. He was so malnourished. If the family had waited much longer, this little guy would have
died. Our hospital took this case as a humanitarian effort since the
family has provided our Special Forces with pertinent information
connected to the Taliban and Al Qaida.

It was about 1430 (2:30 PM), and the baby came rolling through
the TICU doors with the surgeon and anesthesia team at the bedside. Now, remember this is not a "normal" 6-month-old baby, and I
was a little concerned just by the looks on the faces of the anesthesia
team...they looked distressed and worried. During report from the
Certified Registered Nurse Anesthetist (CRNA), he began to discuss
in detail after the surgery was completed, my little patient coded...he
coded right on the operating room table. The anesthesia team initi-

ated chest compressions and began to breathe for the baby with the bag-valve-mask (BVM). The baby's heart rate dipped to a low, deadly point, and without the pediatric advanced life support, this little baby would have died.

As I took down the sides of the crib rails...I quickly glanced at the baby and realized that something was definitely wrong...his color was dusky, and he was working hard to breathe. This little patient had an oral airway in place that was keeping his airway open. As I thought to myself and began to have an internal dialog in my head, "This little baby is coming to me with a piece of plastic in his mouth to help maintain his airway...and when the baby comes out of his sedation, this same piece that is in his mouth is going to stimulate his gag reflex and cause him to vomit and then aspirate into his lungs...and what the fuck...why would the team extubate the baby?"

I stood at the side of the bed, talking to the pediatrician, and asked, "Do you think he should have remained intubated?" The baby had just had oral surgery, and his mouth, tongue, and throat were very swollen...an oral airway will not help long term. He agreed but was not in the OR during the case, so we were trying to manage the baby with what we had.

As I expected, the baby began to decline in health. His color began to worsen, he was gagging, and he could not maintain his own oxygen saturation. The physician ordered me to give Narcan, which is a reversal of the opioids that were given to the baby to medically sedate him. Maybe the baby could not metabolize all the pain and sedation medication due to his less-than-marginal nutritional status. I quickly gave him 10mcg of Narcan and waited. We all waited. And nothing. His status did not improve. As the baby began to worsen, I called out for the code cart and drew up a pediatric dose of epinephrine. The next thing I knew, we were coding the baby...we started to code this little 9-pound baby...I quickly gave the drawn-up epinephrine to the anesthesiologist with no result. His pulse started to drop, and saturation was at 58%.

The anesthesiologist asked for the tools to reintubate the patient...we quickly gathered everything we needed. I had multiple people acting as runners to gather additional items as the doctors yelled out their requirements. We all were determined...I attached the bag-valve-mask (BVM) to the wall O2 and began to breathe for the baby because, at this point, he was no longer breathing on his own. The anesthesia team intubated the baby, but the baby's saturations were still less than what would be expected while on 100 percent oxygen. Needless to say, something was wrong.

Our amazing respiratory team was at the bedside and had the ventilator ready to go...they were ready to attach the machine to the baby, but the anesthesia team was still trying to troubleshoot why the baby's saturations were low.

As the anesthesia team was working on the airway issue, we noticed that the baby's stomach began to get distended, so the surgeon tried to pass a nasogastric tube to decompress the baby's stomach. But nothing would pass through...as the doctors continued to yell for additional equipment, we were all giving our best to save this baby's life. During this time, the doctors were consulting one another and then made the decision to take the baby back to surgery for a much-needed tracheotomy for a more definitive airway in order to save his life.

Once the decision was made to go back to the OR, we were ready to go in seconds; just before we left, one of the technicians grabbed an O2 tank to connect the BVM, which we were using to breathe for the baby. As the CRNA began to connect the BVM, he noticed that somehow the BVM had been disconnected from the wall O2; meaning that we had been bagging the baby on room air. He was upset and just looked at me...he began to yell and belittle me and another technician in the room...in front of everyone. The room was so quiet you could hear a pin drop. At first, I began to beat myself up inside..." How could I let this happen...how stupid could I have been...this baby may now have major brain damage!" As I began to quickly run through the sequence of events in my mind...I remember distinctly connecting the BVM to the wall oxygen because I was the one who initially began to breathe for the baby. I know for certain that the BVM was connected!

This particular CRNA and I do not get along.

He goes to great lengths to belittle me every chance he gets...well, not today, dick! As I stood up to this asshole who just needed someone to blame, I looked at him straight in the face and said, "I don't know if you are trying to point fingers, but I can assure you that the BVM was connected to the wall O2 and was working properly when I first used it when the baby rolled in here. Don't you dare point the finger at me." I had had it...I was DONE! I was sick and tired of him...for some reason, he feels like he is entitled to treat nurses like shit, and what's sad, he is a nurse himself! What we ALL soon realized is that at the time the ventilator was ready to be connected to the baby (but the patient was not ready), the respiratory technician (RT) disconnected the BVM from the wall O2 in order to connect the ventilator, thinking that the baby would be transferred to the vent...however, that did not happen, and the RT forgot to reconnect the BVM.

The baby was quickly taken to the operating room; no sooner than the baby left the ICU, our Radiologist came running through the doors. He asked, "Where is the little baby that was recently intubated!" I told him we had just taken him to the OR for an emergency tracheotomy. He blurted out..." The ET tube is in the esophagus, not in the lungs!" I took off running as fast as I could to the operating room to let the person who confirmed that the ET tube was in the right place was, in fact, in the WRONG position...and that person who confirmed "proper" placement was our wonderful CRNA.

KARMA.

As I informed the CRNA of the incorrect ET placement, he would not even look at me; no wonder the baby did not have good saturations...all the breaths given were going to his little tummy, which was the reason why we couldn't get the nasal gastric tube down and why the baby's abdomen was getting so distended. Talk about karma. Karma is what just bit that CRNA in the ass.

After surgery, I received the baby. He was still extremely ill and unstable, but we made it through. We had a total of 4 codes on this little guy; he has shown me that he is a fighter and will make it through! No matter what the struggle, this little 9-pound baby is determined to make it!

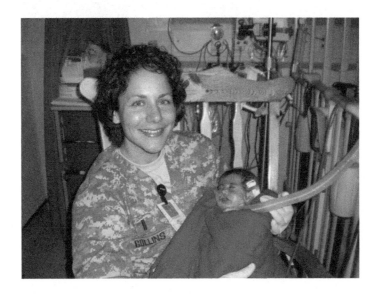

CHRISTINE COLLINS

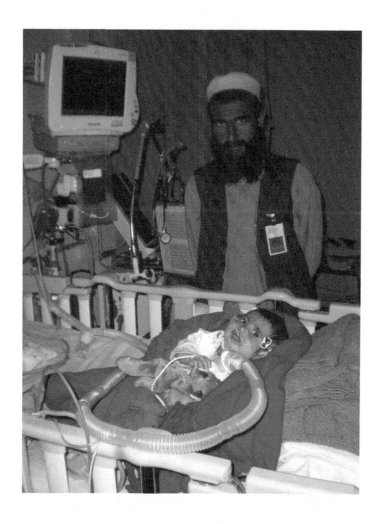

16

— · —

WHERE TO BEGIN

"Keep your face toward the sunshine--and shadows will fall
behind you."
- Walt Whitman

Afghanistan, February 13, 2009

There has been so much that has happened over the past
few days and weeks I just don't know where to begin.

Over the past few days, the weather has been so beautiful. The sun
was out, and there was a cool, crisp breeze in the air. These are the
days that concern a lot of us here...we all know and wonder when
the next massive bombing will occur. We know all too well here that
when nice days come around, the Taliban will make their way out of
the dark, dingy caves to plan their next attack. I never thought in a
million years that I would constantly wish for harsh weather...raining,
snowing, sleet, anything but a beautiful, warm, sunny day.

When my time is up here in Afghanistan, I will never look at warm
sunny days the same. Three days ago, I was called to the ER to help
with a level 1 trauma that was coming in. The Taliban had targeted
our coalition forces. Unfortunately, our coalition members did not do
so well. My patient was in his mid-30s; he was critically injured...head
and face trauma and bilateral lower extremity fractures. He was intu-

bated...it was so hard to see his face from all the blood that was gushing from his mouth, nose, and ears.

As I looked into his mouth to suction the blood out, I noticed that most of his front teeth were floating in the pool of blood that his mouth held. This poor man's jaw was free-floating...he had sustained massive facial injuries. We were not sure if he was going to make it.

As we finished our trauma assessment and stabilized him, we rushed him to CT to get a PAN Scan; his entire body was scanned.

My patient was trying to hang in there...he needed volume to help keep his vital signs stable; we then started to rapidly infuse 4 units of blood and bag after bag of crystalloid products. Just as the scan was completed, we quickly rushed him to the OR for emergency surgery of his lower legs and face. Both legs were fractured, and the right foot had a compound fracture with blood still steadily streaming out from the wound, even with a tourniquet in place. Both of his legs were blue and cold, and I could not feel pedal pulses.

Once the patient was safely in the operating room, I stood outside in the hallway to collect my thoughts and get through all of my charting...as I stood there, I looked up and saw the hospital Chaplain handing over the patient's wedding ring to the patient's guardian, Officer Baguette. It was almost like it happened in slow motion...I could not look away. In a way, the image of that moment took my breath away.

As I stood there, my good friend came up to me and said, "You are going to remember that one, huh." I looked up and just smiled and said, "Yes, I don't know why, but seeing the patient's wedding ring being passed to his guardian meant something to me..." When I saw his wedding ring, I could see this man years before with his soon-to-be bride picking out the "perfect" ring...the ring that he would wear for the rest of his life.

And there we were, just possibly at that point...the point at the end of his life.

I was so saddened by my thoughts and thinking of someone calling his wife to tell her of the horrific news that her husband may not make it. I have only been here for a short 40 days, but I can begin to feel and sense a part of me becoming emotionally detached and numb. I have seen so much and have been a part of something so huge that I really will not know the extent of everything until I return home safely.

I am over worked, over tired, and over stimulated on a daily basis...I can't imagine what I will feel or think at the end of 180 plus days. But what I do know, at this very moment... we have and will continue to do everything for this patient...anything and everything so that he can LIVE...so that this patient can make it home to his wife and live another day.

We all got word that two days ago, there had been multiple suicide bombings in Kabul...I was waiting to see the aftermath of these bombings. It wasn't until today, when I got to work, that our ICU was filled with critically ill patients from this bombing attack, which killed 19 people.

As everyone was buzzing this morning, including myself, I thought quietly...

"Will any of this ever end???"

These patients which we are caring for are incredibly young...they just happened to be in the wrong place at the wrong time. It is hard to look at them because I see their pain and struggles in trying to understand why this has happened.

I am still in disbelief of knowing suicide bombers have and will continue to load up vests full of small, round, solid steel ball bearings and blow themselves up to kill and destroy the masses. I know what this devastation can cause...I have seen it firsthand...I have a patient who cannot talk and cannot respond to me or anyone else because he has two of these solid, steel ball bearings lodged into his brain...this boy's prognosis is not good.

In addition, I have been taking care of two men...one is a local Afghan police officer who was blown up by a different suicide bomber about 4 days ago. This patient has major head trauma and has lost his lower leg on the right side. The other leg is being held together with pins, screws, and metal plates. This patient continues to bleed from both his legs, and we have been routinely transfusing him with blood products just to keep his hemoglobin and hematocrit somewhat at a low "normal" level.

My other patient is intubated; he was shot by a member of the Taliban. The gunshot wound entered his left flank and exited through his right flank as the bullet traveled through his body, severing his bowels. Yesterday, he was on several different drips to keep his blood pressure up; he was sedated and in shock. Today, he went back to surgery to repair the massive bowel injury and now has a colostomy. We were able to get him extubated by the end of the shift; that means he is getting better, and I was excited to see that.

It has been snowing since last night; there is snow every-where...parts of the airfield are closed, and I could care less if it snows every day while I am here.... Being that it is snowing, there will be fewer bombings and killings.

As I wind down from another stressful and outrageous day, I begin to look back at my week starting from Sunday...over the past 5 days, I have worked a total of 82 hours... and as I place my head on my pillow, I will be ready to work another 26 hours over the next two days.

Where to begin...and when will it end?

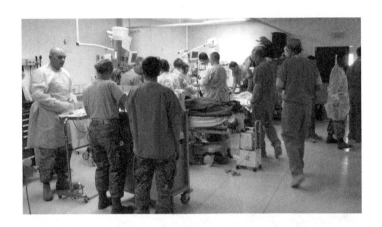

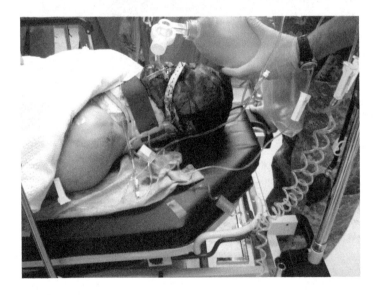

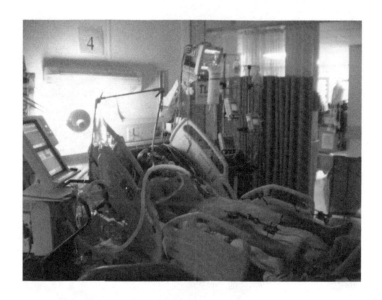

17

— • —

A PHONE CALL HOME

"I am only one, but I am one. I cannot do everything, but I can do something. And I will not let what I cannot do interfere with what I can do."
—— Edward Everett Hale

Afghanistan, February 15, 2009

Today was a good day...a good day to the end of 108 hours of work in a 6-day stretch.

Everyone is tired and wants just one day to sleep in. Well, I get my chance tomorrow...I think I will sleep the entire day away. Today was my fourth-day taking care of a local Afghan police officer who was on a mission and was involved in an IED explosion. The magnitude of the blast was so strong that it blew the lower half of his left leg completely off, and he sustained major trauma to the right lower extremity, which required extensive surgery to save. This man has been with us for the past 5 days. Initially, he was intubated and on life support. We didn't get much in the report when we received him; all we knew was that he was a local police officer who survived this horrific blast, and now he was here with us to help save his life and limbs.

After he was extubated 3 days ago, he was confused and combative. He would yell out and begin to thrash about in the bed. He was a handful full, to say the least. Most nurses would sedate him. However, he also suffered severe head trauma, which he was recovering from as well. I made a conscious decision to NOT sedate him, and I was willing to accept all repercussions that came with that decision. I wondered what was going on in this patient's head. I wondered if he knew where he was, if he knew that he was safe...being that the patient had been sedated, there was no tangible way to tell if he was with it or not.

At one point during my day with him, he swung to hit me in the face and began to yell. I quickly called for an interpreter so that they could explain to me what he was saying. Apparently, he thought I was a member of the Taliban, and we were in a gunfight; he was yelling for his weapon and telling me to leave. I could completely understand because his last conscious memory was being blown up. I stood firmly and explained to this 21-year-old man that he was safe and that he was in the intensive care unit at Bagram. It took a while, but he tired himself out and finally fell back asleep. It took three full days of dealing with his outbreaks of rage, but finally... yesterday...the roughness of his face and the madness in his eyes faded away. I slowly approached him and touched his bloody and bruised arm. I smiled at him and told him that he was safe and he would be okay. He just looked at me and smiled...then, out of nowhere, he gave me the "thumbs-up" sign. I just laughed, and he smiled. As I quickly called an interpreter to the bedside, I began to ask him if he remembered what happened to him and if he knew where he was. He was able to answer a few questions but just couldn't remember in detail about the explosion...he would tire very easily, so I let him rest just before I left his bedside. I asked him about his family. Come to find out, he is married and has a small daughter...of course, I began to wonder if they even knew he was alive. My mind began to race for ways to contact his family...I quickly asked him for his home number, but he was unable to remember all the numbers. We still called 7 to 8 different phone numbers just to give it a try, with no success.

I waited until today...my 21-year-old police officer was doing much better. He was so kind and gentle...he was equally grateful...it felt good to be genuinely appreciated. As we talked and I fed him, I asked him if he could remember what his home phone number was. You could see him struggling to remember. The interpreter wrote down six different numbers and none of them worked. We gave it one last shot, and finally...as we dialed the last phone number, there was a voice on the other line. I wasn't sure if it was the right number...so I waited until I could understand the response of the person on the other line. As the interpreter began to talk, I soon realized we had the right number! All I could hear on the other end of the phone was a man crying. The father was overjoyed that his son was still alive.

No one knew where this 21-year-old was...they thought he had died in the IED explosion and were all devastated. When my patient spoke to his father for the first time, he broke down in tears. They both cried on the phone. I felt renewed. I felt the compassion and caring that I once felt when I got here 42 days ago all rushed back inside of my body, from the top of my head to the bottom of my toes.

I felt that no matter what I did for the rest of the day, *THIS was* my highlight!

This small phone call home made the difference...it made the difference in multiple lives that I will never know the true impact. I was so excited...my patient's father will be coming to see his son for the first time on Tuesday.

I look forward to this family reunion, just like I look forward to my own in July. As my patient hung up the phone, my eyes began to tear up, and I had the biggest smile on my face.

I made a difference today.

18

A WEEK OF MANY THANKS

**"Gratitude can transform common days into thanksgiving, turn
routine jobs into joy and change ordinary opportunities into
blessings"**
— William Arthur Ward

Afghanistan, February 23, 2009

At the start of my work week, I was sitting quietly in the
TICU break room, trying to eat my lunch quickly, when Nazir, one of
our interpreters, came to me and said that he had something for me.

I said, "You have something for meeeee??" with a big smile on my
face.

At first, my mind was going in circles. "What could he possibly have
for me?" I got up quickly from my chair, and as I passed the threshold
of the break room door, where Nazir stood, I could see a tall, thin man
behind him. I looked at him, and my eyebrows frowned in confusion
because I wasn't sure who or what this man needed. But, as I got closer
and could see this man's face clearer, within seconds, I knew who this
man was.

The man standing before me was the same man I heard on the
telephone last week crying out for his son because he thought that his
son was dead. They looked just like each other.

My face beaming with light, I quickly walked to him with my hands out to shake his hand. The man smiled, all the while, as the interpreter explained to him who I was. My next question to the father was, "Have you seen your son yet?" Without words being said, he quickly shook his head no. I then said, "Well, what are we waiting for? Your son has been waiting for you for a long time."

As we walked down the hall to the TICU, I was the first to enter the patient's room. The patient had a big smile on his face, and with his right hand touching the left side of his chest over his heart, he nodded his head as a thank you and welcome. I did the same with my right hand over my heart as he looked at me. I could tell that something had caught his eye behind me. I just smiled and moved to the side.

He saw his dad for the first time in 4 weeks.

They greeted one another with shaky voices and even some tears. After the greetings were over, both the patient and father thanked me. I was so happy to be a part of this wonderful reunion. It filled my heart with warmth and goodness.

As the days passed this week, I will always remember the many thanks from the people I have had the privilege and honor to help. All these moments will forever be rooted in my memory. There will be many times like these I will need to draw strength upon as I continue my time in Afghanistan. I will cherish these memories, the memories of a father and son, just as I will cherish the thank you from France.

I was notified that I needed to attend a meeting with some distinguished visitors from Paris, France. I could feel the excitement in the air from all those who were going to be in attendance. There were going to be several French officers coming from Kabul to thank our trauma team who saved one of their men on February 13, 2009.

The time was 1100, and everyone began to gather in the operating room since the OR was the only place big enough to hold so many people. As everyone gathered, I had the opportunity to greet our distinguished visitors at the hospital entrance with the Deputy Commander, the Superintendent Chief, and the Executive Officer. I was excited to meet these men and hear how our patient was recovering back in Paris. I was hoping for good news that he was still alive and safe.

As we escorted our distinguished visitors to the OR, we walked down the same hall where I stood weeks ago, caring for this French soldier and watching as our Chaplain passed his wedding ring to the patient's French guardian for safekeeping. The French Colonel began to speak, conveying his gratitude and goodwill. He then provided everyone with an update, which was the update I had been waiting for.

The colonel said that the French soldier was still fighting for his life, that he had a rough uphill battle, but that he was continuing to fight to stay alive. We all begin to clap and cheer to know that he is still alive and fighting.

Just after the medical update, the French Colonel then presented a beautiful silver thank-you Medallion to our Deputy commander on behalf of the French Army. We all were just blown away; it was such a nice token of appreciation, but the French colonel was not done. The French Colonel had another gift, and as I stood there, my name was called.

The colonel presented me with the gift for providing outstanding nursing care that greatly contributed to the overall well-being of this French soldier.

"Many thanks," said the colonel as he handed me a beautiful carved wooden box with the silver coin at the top right corner of the box that said, "Service de Sante des Armees." Inside the box is a hand-carved

wooden pen trimmed in the same silver that the coin was made from.
I was honored to receive such a gift.

What a week.

A week of many thanks.

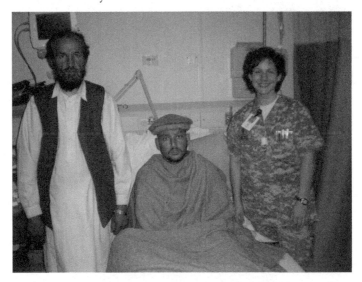

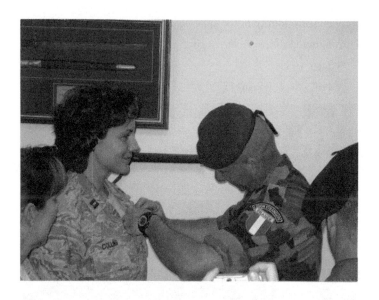

The AMAZING, LTC Elizabeth Coddington, Trauma Critical Care
Unit Commander and Collins

19

— . —

ROSE COLORED GLASSES

"I have found the paradox, that if you love until it hurts, there can be no more hurt, only more love."
-Mother Teresa

Afghanistan, March 2, 2009

I'd like to think during some of my time here that I will wear rose-colored glasses instead of focusing on the travesty and devastation that surrounds this place.

At times, I particularly like to put my rose-colored glasses on when I care for some of our enemy combatants. It never ceases to amaze me how a person's outlook or perception, combined with the simple human touch, can be so powerful. More powerful than one can comprehend at times. Today, I took care of another enemy combatant. We currently have several in our unit.

Just last week, he and his friend were injured in a gunfight just outside of our base. The enemy combatants were targeting an American convoy. My patient's friend was not so lucky; he died a few days ago. The friend was gravely injured, and a bullet severed his spinal cord. We waited 2 days to see if the patient would respond, but no response was given from this dying patient.

Therefore, we disconnected the ventilator and gave orders to push IV morphine until he quietly passed away.

As I stood next to this enemy combatant, I could see the color slowly fade from his body and his soul gently drift away. While I watched the dying process take place, I continued to pray for him as he left this Earth to go to a better place. I quietly thought to myself that this dead man was probably indeed the fortunate one, the fortunate one to have escaped this war-torn country.

As I began my shift taking care of another enemy combatant, I noticed that there was much nursing care that had been neglected over the last few days. I understand that this man was captured after shooting at our own soldiers, but where is the humanity in all of this?

As I drew some warm bath water, my patient began to beg me for a drink. He had been shot in the back and was now paralyzed. He had a collapsed lung, chest tubes, and multiple drains coming from his abdomen due to an open abdominal surgical incision that was the full length of his torso. The man was injured by a high-velocity rifle that ripped part of his diaphragm apart and hit his spinal column.

This man was in bad shape.

When he would look at me, I could not see the bad, nor could I see that he was an "enemy combatant." My rose-colored glasses would not allow it. All I could see was a thin and fragile man that lay before me who looked sad and so ashamed. Initially he asked if I would call his family, but then changed his mind because he did not want them to know what he had done.

As I took my time caring for him, giving him a much-needed bath, brushing his teeth, washing his hair, changing his sheets, and giving him small pieces of ice to help moisten his mouth, he began to come alive and smiled.

What is amazing to me is that just a few short days ago, if this man were standing next to me just outside our base, he would have killed me without a second thought.

The other nurses, at times, become frustrated with me because I tend to care too much. What I believe is that we, as nurses, are here to do a job. We may not like or agree on who we care for, but it is our personal responsibility and obligation to give the best care possible, whether they are Americans, Coalition forces, local Nationals, and even enemy combatants. This is what we have trained for. Everything that we have done in our lives has prepared us for this one moment. This moment and giving our best to our patients without judgment or personal biases. After all, this man was still someone's son, someone's grandson, someone's dad, someone's nephew.

It's fucked up, I know. But to get through today, right now... I like my rose-colored glasses, and I will make sure to carry them everywhere I go.

I will soon be leaving Bagram Air Base. I will be exploring a different place in Afghanistan. I have been selected to travel outside the wire to a small forward operating base 90 miles outside the Iranian border, working in conjunction with the Special Operations team. I am privileged to have been given the opportunity to continue to make a difference here in Afghanistan to support traveling medical convoy missions to small villages caring for women and children.

I understand and accept the level of danger that goes along with these missions. Both Clinton and I have discussed this decision in detail, and he has and always will continue to be my strongest supporter.

Clinton knows me so well.

He knows that I need to do this not only for myself but for those lives I will touch and make a difference. My travels will take me well into the end of March. I look forward to the new and challenging events that will come my way. All the while, I continue to do my part in this war, while persevering to be a bright light to those who are affected by this war-stricken country.

20

— . —

TALIBAN AT THE GATES

A fghanistan, March 3, 2009

The news hit the wire...

BBC News 3 Mar 2009

"Blasts target main US Afghan base"

The US military says two bomb blasts near the gate to its main Afghan base have injured at least three people.

A car bombing outside the Bagram base was followed moments later by a suicide bombing, US officials said. "No US soldier was present at that moment, but three contractors have suffered minor injuries," a US military spokesman told the AFP news agency. Bagram Air Base is about 60km (40 miles) north of Kabul. It is the main base for the US-led coalition force.

"There were two explosions, first a vehicle and then a suicide bomber wearing an explosives vest, near the gate," Sergeant First Class Joel Peavey told AFP. Military officials also said that three NATO soldiers had been killed after being wounded in a bomb blast in the south on Tuesday.

Taliban insurgency:

Originally built by the Soviet military during its invasion of Afghanistan in the 1980s, some 10,000 troops are based at Bagram.

They are mostly Americans but also include French, Egyptian, New Zealand, Turkish, German, and Australian troops serving as part of the coalition. In addition, the base houses the US military's main prison facility in Afghanistan for people detained by US forces.

The latest deaths in the south take the number of international soldiers killed in Afghanistan this year to 52, according to the casualties.org website that tracks casualties in Afghanistan. NATO has not divulged the identities of the dead soldiers or the exact location of the attack, but a Canadian general has been reported by the AP news agency as saying that they were all Canadian. The south of Afghanistan has become the center of the Taliban insurgency after they were forced from power by US-led forces in 2001."

They say that being a nurse doesn't have its dangers. They say that being in the safety of a big base doesn't have its dangers. They say that this far south we'd be safe and doesn't have its dangers. The blast was right outside our base. The identities of the dead soldiers that NATO has not divulged, according to this article?

They were my patients, and I'll never forget their faces.

There's a surreal quality to reading this article, which doesn't show the ugliness of war. It doesn't show the faces of war. It's black and white words on a piece of paper. They can't honestly portray the fear, the grief, the sense of living each day on a razor's edge, never knowing when the next blast might shatter the fragile illusion of safety.

I think of that Canadian soldier, his body broken and his heart shattered by the loss of his friends. I think of how he opened up to me, how we cried together, two strangers bound by the weight of all we had seen and carried.

Life happens in all its beauty and all its brutality. We cannot control the bombs that go off, the loved ones we lose, and the dreams that shatter in the face of reality. But we can control how we respond. We can choose to reach out, to connect, to find solace and strength in the shared experience of being human.

It's not easy.

And yet, here we are.

Still standing, still breathing, still finding the courage to keep going.

21

— . —

IED Hunters

"Life happened. In all its banality, brutality, cruelty, unfairness. But also in its beauty, pleasures, and delights. Life happened"
— Thrity Umrigar, author and journalist

Afghanistan, March 4, 2009

My patient now is a Canadian Coalition forces member who has been deployed to Afghanistan since January 2008. He and his team members are like brothers. They have done everything together. They eat together, play together, work together, and even sleep together.

Now, they have shared the loss of life together.

This particular five-man team's job is to find and detonate IEDs located in specific parts of Afghanistan. Their vehicle is well equipped, including a robot that is used to recover and detonate IEDs when found. These men are silent Heroes because they do a job that most cannot. They are in the business of bomb recovery so that others can live. In my opinion, they are saving future lives of Americans, Coalition forces, and even local Nationals.

As I walked into the patient's room to get a report from the off-going nurse (one of our unit "murses," which means a male nurse, who is as lazy as they come), I could see my newly admitted patient with a half-smile on his face, as if he's trying to get through the off-going nurses bullshit questions.

The off-going nurse said something to the effect, "Lt. Collins, this is the only thermometer in the unit. Please don't lose it." I looked at the off-going Army nurse, rolled my eyes, and said, "So what you're saying is lose the only thermometer the unit has? Isn't it time for you to get off of work already?"

My patient looked at me, and just started laughing. He laughed so much that his chest hurt, and all he said was, "All right I can see that you and I are meant for each other!"

I just said, "You got it," and then I replied, "Now, back to the important stuff. My name is Christine, and I'm going to be your crazy nurse for the evening, so make sure your seat is in the upright position with your tray table locked and securely fastened."

It was nice to make my patient laugh. He needed to feel good, even if it was just for a moment. After all, he had just been blown up by an IED and lost three of his best men.

For the other nursing staff, he was noticeably quiet and, at times, shutting down. After the laughter was gone, and I started the IV pump to give him his first round of antibiotics, I pulled up a chair and just sat at the foot of his bed. I wanted to make sure that he had someone there to talk to if he wanted to talk.

At first, he was quiet, but then he began to open up.

He just looked at me with his blue eyes filled with tears and said, "This is it; this is reality, right? This just happened. God, I cannot believe it, one of my absolute best friends is gone. You know, I have known him for 20 years. He has four children. Oh my God, do you think their families have even been notified?"

I reached for my patient's hand and told him that all the notifications had been taken care of. He then began to use his right arm, the best he could, which was severely injured, and tried to draw a diagram of his vehicle on top of his bandage so that I could understand where everyone was sitting just before the explosion.

As reality began to sink in further, I could see in his eyes a look of devastation. There was a sense of solitude that overcame his body. He went over and over the events that took place as if somehow things could have been different.

He began to tell me that his driver only suffered a few small bumps and bruises. The patient himself ended up with bilateral broken clavicles, multiple rib fractures, pulmonary contusions, and a badly fractured right hand.

His friend who sat behind him was fatally injured and passed away shortly after the explosion.

However, the two other men who sat toward the back of the vehicle were instantly incinerated. "My men didn't even have a chance. They didn't even know what hit them. All I saw was a spray of pink mist from their bodies being blown up."

My patient then closed his eyes and began to shake his head from left to right. I moved closer to my patient's bed, and I held his hand. I began to shed a few tears and said how sorry I was, and I wish there were something I could do or say that would fix the events that took place just less than 24 hours ago. He then begins to question life and why did three of his men have to die. "If I had been sitting one seat over, it would have been me...It would have been me, the one who would have died." He went on, "Who makes this decision? Who's the one that says you can live, but you three cannot?"

As I quietly sat next to him, I just shook my head up and down and said, "You are right. There is no rhyme or reason for this war. No one really knows when it is their turn. However, you must have been meant for something great. You are alive. You are here. You are safe with me now. You are the one that has been given a second chance."

As we sat together, my heart was wide open. We continued to talk and cry together.

Before I knew it, it was shift change.

The night shift nurse came into the room to get report, and I handed over the only thermometer in the unit. I smiled at my patient; he smiled back. I reminded him that he was meant to do remarkable things. Whether he realized it or not, he survived for a reason. He was meant to live so that he could change many lives for the better. He smiled, and we hugged. I told him that I was immensely proud of him and that he did the absolute best job he could for himself but, most importantly, for his men. Soon after we talked, my patient was air-evacuated to Germany for further care.

At the end of my shift, one of the nurses called out to me. But they didn't call me Collins; they called me 'Florence' or 'Flo,' for short. The nurse began to tell me how proud she was to work with me. She said that since I have been here that I continue to inspire her, and others around us. She continued to recognize me for my compassion and my ability to care even in the face of devastation. She thanked me for making a difference, and I replied, "After all, isn't that what we are here for? Right?"

As the weather continues to get warmer and the insurgents in the Taliban become stronger, we will be increasingly under attack.

Today, our base was attacked and bombed twice. The suicide bomber and a vehicle-born IED were detonated just outside our main gate. These bombings are a wake-up call to many of us here on base.

We are closer to war and death than most people realize. Bagram continues to be one of the key bases in Afghanistan, and it's become clear to everyone that this will be one hotspot over the next several months. As I prepare to fly out tomorrow to Farah, I will keep all of you close to my heart.

22

—·—

PROVING MYSELF

"It always seems impossible until it's done."
--Nelson Mandela

Afghanistan, March 11, 2009

Coming to Farah, I never thought that I would have to prove myself to anyone. In my mind I thought I would come here to do nursing work and nursing work alone.

However, much to my surprise I forgot entirely what it was like to train and work with the Army. Being here for only 24 hours is taking me back to 14 years ago. A time when I first trained with Special Forces at Fort Dix, New Jersey. For me, at the time, I was 20 years old and wanted to conquer the world.

The Army's Air Base Ground Defense training lasted over a month with Special Forces. I was taught never to give up, and when I felt like I was going to give up, well, that was just not an option. I pushed myself through 6 weeks of hell, pushing myself to the point of no return. Being put through situations and obstacles that one would think she would never get out of, or better yet, survive. But I always did... I always did survive. At the end of my training at Fort Dix, I was proud of what I accomplished.

Here in Farah, I am with a team of eight people, myself included. I am the only female Air Force member in an eight-man team in the middle of nowhere. After flying in on the 10th of March, on a dirt runway, it was only a short 3 hours later that I found myself running 4.7 miles around the same dirt runway which I had just landed.

Simply put, it's the Army way.

Today, I met with the physician that approached me on doing a MEDCAP (medical convoy), which is a mobile clinic reaching out to the locals and providing much needed medical care. Our discussion became more in-depth, and time flew by. I could see the guys getting ready for physical training. I wanted to go, but then again, I did not want to go. My body needed rest from the 4.7 miles we had run the day before.

The leader of our team said to me, "Are you coming? You know you can come with us." I said, "No, that's okay; I want to talk to the physician regarding our upcoming mission." I felt bad for trying to get out of the run, which was planned, but my body is not what it used to be 15 years ago. I felt beat down like an older woman with major physical limits.

As the next 15 minutes went by, I just couldn't take it anymore. I had to go and meet up with the rest of my team. I continued to tell myself, "What a little bitch. These are your teammates. You can't let them down. What they do, you do, end of story."

So, I ran quickly to my room, leaving my uniform on and placing my 45-pound body armor on. I strapped my 9mm Beretta on my shoulder holster and four magazine clips with a total of 60 rounds in place and began to run the dirt road to catch up with the rest of my teammates.

As I began to run, I could immediately feel the pressure of my body armor and additional pack on my lower back, and all I could think was,

"Thank God I took Tylenol tablets before I left my room!" I really didn't know where the guys went, but I was going to that same dirt flight line to see if they were there. Sure enough, in the far distance, I could barely make out the silhouettes of my team members.

At first, I thought there was no way I could catch up, but then I just did it.

I grabbed the top of my body armor that rested on my shoulders, holding on to my 9 mm and bullets, and I just started running. I ran until I couldn't run anymore, and then I started to walk. Once I caught my breath, I started to run repeatedly. I kept thinking about my husband, Clinton, who has just been running for me. I thought if he could do it, then I could do it, too, so I just did it.

Finally, after 2 miles, I caught up with the rest of my team members. Once the guys realized that it was me running to them, they all stopped in disbelief. They couldn't believe it; they were shocked. As I got closer, I could hear them all clapping and putting their hands up to give me high fives. It felt really good. Even though my body was aching, my belt had cut into my lower back, which at this point was now bleeding, and my feet were burning due to newly acquired blisters from my combat boots, but I felt good.

I proved myself. Without saying a word, these men knew I was tough. And that I would not give up on myself, but more importantly, I would never give up on them.

2009, Farah, Afghanistan

2009, Farah, Afghanistan. The Army Way

2009, Farah, Afghanistan, Proving myself

23

FARAH FREE CLINIC

"If you can tune into your purpose and really align with it,
setting goals so that your vision is an expression of that purpose,
then life flows much more easily."
———Jack Canfield

Afghanistan, March 12, 2009

Today was my first day to experience the free clinic in Farah.
I must say that I was amazed and overwhelmed all in the same way.
I felt so good to be here...to be a part of this wonderful experience.
Picture, if you will, a remote desert village surrounded by beautiful,
large, jagged mountains sprouting from the earth's core. I love it here.
The village itself is exceedingly small with no running water and sand
being tossed around with the slightest breeze. The people in this area
are small, malnourished, and have not bathed in quite some time. The
children are dirty and underdeveloped...they all are innocent, with
gleaming smiles that cover their faces...especially when they see me.
The younger girls were amazed that a woman was waiting for them,
assessing them, and treating them for their illness...all the young girls
were so excited.

The women look much older than they actually are due to their
tough, rugged lifestyle and the culture into which they were born.

As I entered my designated clinic room where I would see all the women and children, I became overwhelmed with emotion...not of sadness but of joy and a sense of pride and responsibility. This overwhelming sense of responsibility came with me as wanting to make a small difference to these women and children...to make a difference in their lives...to make a difference in this small part of the world. Most of the young girls looked at me in amazement, for they rarely see a woman in my position...all the young girls were giggling and excited to allow me to listen to their heartbeat with my stethoscope. Moreover, they were all pleased when I was able to treat some of their conditions with much-needed antibiotics, Tylenol, Pedialyte, nutritional supplements, and vitamins. These patients felt like they were being heard...that their pain and suffering would be somewhat delayed for the moment.

By the end of my clinic day, which only lasted from 0930 to 1100, I was able to see and treat 15 children ranging from the age of 3 months to 12 years old and 6 women. As my work here in Farah continues, my respect for women and the lives they live continues to grow leaps and bounds. I will forever be grateful for what I have in the United States and the lives that Clinton and I provide for our three daughters. One day, I will teach and show my daughters how others live, not by choice but by birth. I will teach them how lucky they are to have been born in such a great country...a country that respects women...represents freedom and opportunity.

I am grateful and reminded on a daily basis of how blessed I am.

As my day continued to wind down, I went for a walk in our small one-mile by one-mile compound; I heard over my handheld radio, "All Medics Las Vegas, I repeat, Las Vegas." I quickly ran to the makeshift hospital; I knew there was a Level 1 trauma coming in.

As I came into the trauma bay, I gathered my nursing items and began to prep my assigned bay...we had two fresh traumas come through
the door, which was involved in a motor vehicle crash. They were both
somewhat stable but had head trauma...their vehicle was traveling
over 90 mph when it crashed into a concrete wall...both men hit the
dashboard and windshield with their heads. We quickly evaluated and
treated both patients, provided IV fluids, stabilized the patients, and
then transferred them out to the Farah hospital for further care within
hours.

Today has been a day of many challenges, both happy and stressful...as I continue my time here in Farah, I will make each day count,
and I will continue to give a small part of myself to those I serve.

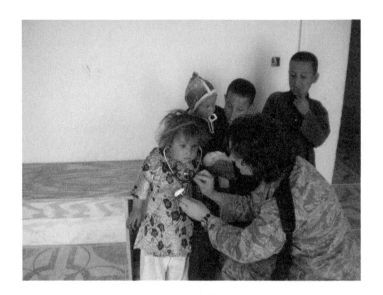

24

— • —

THE SMELL OF ROTTING FLESH

"Life is pleasant. Death is peaceful. It's the transition that's
troublesome."
—— Isaac Asimov

A fghanistan, March 17, 2009

The smell hit the doorway before the patient did.

As this elderly-looking woman entered my room, I could see the
swarm of flies that imprisoned her body. They flew around her head,
in her face, mouth, and shoulders, but more specifically, the left side
of her upper body. The stench was so bad that most people left the
room. As I stood there, taking care of the children who came into my
assigned clinic room along with their mothers.

I could see the faces of my interpreter and her mother...the look of
disgust and irritation.

People shunned this 40-something-year-old woman; no one would
speak to her...she looked homeless and destitute. I quickly finished my
patients and then devoted my time and attention to this woman, who
looked like she had lived an extremely hard and tough life...as she sat
before me, she began to cry. I kneeled and held her hand...making sure
that I was breathing through my mouth because I had almost vomited

once already due to the smell. She began to point at her left breast, which was very painful and much larger than her right.

As I helped her remove her dress, I saw something...something that will be remembered always, including the smell that was burnt in my nares with every small and faint breath I took.

This woman who sat before me had stage 4 breast cancer. You did not need a fancy CT scan, MRI, not even a biopsy to determine her fate. This woman's left breast was overrun with cancer...so much so that her left breast appeared to be the size of a DD, which was hollowed out with a large crater in the middle of her breast, and the inside bones of her chest wall could be seen.

As I began to remove more of the dressings this woman had placed around her breast, I began to notice that with every slight pull of the cloth, her skin would simply "fall off." Her breast was fire engine red, but no blood drained from the site...the cancer had taken over that part of the body's blood supply, all the surrounding tissue, and now had become necrotic.

The tissue...the tissue to the opening of the large crater that filled the middle of her breast was almost like clumps of cottage cheese that would come apart with the smallest touch.

This poor woman in her 40s, who looked much like in her 70s, with a long, dark, drained face, her eyes had sunken in so much that they sat far back into her skull, with her cheekbones so drawn in that her face looked like a skeleton...she sat there but with only a few teeth in her mouth and was sobbing.

She was sobbing that she was in pain and had many large "bumps" that tracked up her left armpit, and she wanted to take something to "fix it." I sat calmly, held her hand...I listened to every one of her concerns. I knew in my heart that there was nothing I or anyone else could do for her. I knew what truly mattered at this point was my approach, kindness, and compassion for this lonely woman who was probably going to die alone.

It took me only a few moments to draw up a shot of antibiotics...which I then gave to her in the fattiest part of her body, her buttocks...even then, her skin just sagged over her body like an oversized coat.

As she lay on my wooden bench, I helped her up...she was sitting up, and that's when the real work began.

I took my time. I carefully inspected her breast, looking for maggots that may have developed a home within her open chest and body...I wasn't surprised when I didn't find any. If I had found them, at least it would have been a good sign...at least I would have known that the maggots were eating the infected tissue and leaving behind new, clean skin. However, that was not the case; all that was found was dead, necrotic skin.

I began to pack her open wound with a wet-to-dry dressing and carefully wrapped her entire upper chest wall with Kerlix. I wanted to make sure that she had enough dressing to absorb all the liquid skin that was sloughing off her body. I only wished that there was something I could have done with the smell.

Gosh, that smell...I cannot even imagine what that would be like, to have to live with myself or a person I loved with this condition. It is a condition in the US that could be easily corrected and treated, but here, it is almost unheard of. In these parts of the world, medical care is a rarity...it is as if they live back in the 1300's.

I must say, after several minutes of being in the closed room with this woman, it seemed as if, somehow, I became immune to the stench.

I made sure that the women knew I accepted her as is and that she was always welcomed back. After her antibiotics were administered, her dressing was completed, she received all her supplies, we made sure she had a follow-up appointment for next Tuesday, and I placed my right hand over my heart, saying, "Tashaqure," which means Thank You.

As another busy day began to wind down, I had been up for a total of 32 hours, and it was only 1:00 in the afternoon when a small child caught my eye. I asked who the child was and what she needed. I was told that her father had brought her in because she was very ill. Over the past two years, she started vomiting and became constipated with little to no growth. The father began to tell his story in which he had sold everything to get his daughter medical attention and that his family had no more money. The only thing the family had left was a cow, which they would milk to sell for money. Now, the father had to sell the cow to help pay for medical expenses for his daughter.

Here in this country, females are not favored.

Most daughters are given in marriage by the time they are 12 years old to men who are 3 to 4 times their age...it makes my stomach churn just thinking about it. We decided to take the child and her father back to our base and provide further examinations. Any chance of sleeping was a far distant thought...there was work to be done, and I wanted to make sure that I could be this little girl's advocate.

Through the many gates and body searches, the little girl and her father finally made it to our small, garage-like hospital. We began immediately with x-rays, x-rays with contrast, blood work, etc....there was a long wait. It became clear with the x-ray results that there was some type of blockage... which required further investigation. However, Farah is definitely not the right place for this type of treatment and or care. What this little girl needed was a scope of her esophagus; however, we were not equipped for this type of procedure.

We are a "Forward Surgical Team" with Special Operations...we didn't have the equipment for this, nor did anyone around Farah.

As I watched the young child sit on the floor, my mind began to wonder...I felt like I was in a different place, a different time; in my mind, I was with my own three daughters...I could imagine one of them being sick and talking to their doctor. I could see in my mind that my own children would be okay. No matter what, they would remain healthy and safe because of the type of medical care we are fortunate to have at our fingertips. This place... this place here is so different...children are considered lucky if they survive until their teenage years. Then, my attention was taken away from my own thoughts of my children to the child's father's cry for help.

As the interpreter began to speak for him...he started telling the story of having no money and hardly any food...this is a story that I hear daily from all Afghans I meet. A story in which I am not sure who is telling the truth and who lies to take advantage of the Americans who desperately want to provide assistance. But, this father, this child, they were different...their eyes were the windows to their souls.

As the father began to speak...I believed him; I really knew that he loved his daughter, and he wanted her well...that he would continue to do everything he could to help his daughter get better. My mind raced...I wanted to help. I quickly ran to my room and got some cash. All I could find was $12.00; I shoved the two 5's and two 1's into my pocket and went back to the hospital.

I began to pace...I didn't want anyone to see me give this man and his daughter the money, so I waited. I waited until the right moment, and there it was; we were getting ready to take the father and daughter back to the gate that separated their village from our base. I motioned the father to me with a wave of my hand, and I neatly folded the money and handed it to him.

There was a look of surprise and gratitude that came over the harsh overtones of his face; he then began to smile with delight and stated over and over again, "Tashaqure," "Tashaqure," while placing his hand over his heart. Eventually, one of the physicians found a hospital in Kabul that would be willing to take the daughter and complete the much-needed tests so that this child could hopefully become healthy. We will follow up with her in the next few weeks. I am looking forward to seeing her and her recovery...I look forward to seeing a healthy 12-year-old girl who can remain a child.

25

THE FARAH EXPERIENCE

"Do not go where the path may lead, go instead where there is
no path and leave a trail."
- Ralph Waldo Emerson

A fghanistan, April 2, 2009

As the plane landed on the dirt runway in the wild west of Farah, Afghanistan; I never imagined what experiences would be waiting for me...waiting for me to see, touch, feel and be a part of. When that plane came to a stop on March the 10th, I could see my new teammates lined up by an ambulance waiting to pick me up...those same individuals would be the "Band of Brothers" that I would now call family.

Once the dust settled on the dirt runway in Farah and the plane was finally at a standstill...waiting for the engines to stop roaring...I peered out of my window one last time and felt an overwhelming feeling of uncertainty. A surge of mixed emotions came over me... "Will I be safe?" "Will I get hurt?" "What will I see?" and "What will happen here," the strongest of them was uncertainty. I took a deep breath, got off the plane, and was determined to make my mark here in the Wild West. Without a second thought, I packed my mixed emotions away in my suitcase...I didn't have time to deal with them; I humbly stepped off that plane, and then the introductions began, and off to work I went...

Two names I will forever remember...Capt Tulp and Sgt Cauley; all I can say when I think of them is outstanding.

What exceptional team leaders...these two individuals alone have created a pleasant and warm atmosphere for everyone...as if we lived in a magical time and place. A time and place that I did not want to leave. They cared about each of us, but more importantly, they cared about the "team." They instilled in each of us that we have a vital role, which is crucial to our overall capability as a team for saving lives...each of us had a job, and we did it well.

Both Capt Tulp and Sgt Cauley are dazzling individuals which sets the example for others to follow. I can only hope to be half of what these two individuals are...to be a brilliant leader in the future.

They are the driving force for the synergistic effect that bonds our team together.

Our team is composed of 8 people; we are a Forward Surgical Team (FST)...we have one surgeon, one CRNA, two surgical techs, one LPN, two critical care RNs, and an NCOIC. We are as far forward as you can be to the war, and we are reminded of that fact daily. From traumas that roll through the doors to the equipment, which is moved from place to place, the missions that take place in the middle of the night, to the intelligence received daily, reminding us of the constant threat on our small forward operating base.

We are a small, tight-knit group that I am so proud to have been a part of. I feel a strong kinship with these brothers...we have been through something together that will forever bind us. From the traumas that would take us into 24 to sometimes 36-hour workdays, to the days at the Farah Free Clinic...the children that would smile and giggle when they would see us and stare in amazement that a woman was caring for them. My brothers were always constant supporters, encouraging one another to get through one more day together.

When I was notified on March 30th that I would be leaving Farah, I once again felt a mix of emotions that flooded my heart and mind. No longer was the feeling of uncertainty, but of the sadness of letting go...this place has left an imprint on my heart that I will think of every passing day until I reach the end of my road in life. I am overcome with sadness when I think that I will not be here to help the locals at the clinic...from this point on, I will see the faces of the children and their mothers only in my dreams. My hopes and fears will come to pass in my absences for those who will live another day and the others who inevitably will die.

Being here, being a part of the Farah experience, has opened my already widened eyes to so much more. I think about the tragedy of this country and the many wars and invasions this country has endured. Even with the years of so-called "progress," it remains so subtle that one could "overlook" the progress by sheer accident. The people still live in mud huts with no electricity or running water, and medical care is a rare commodity that is almost unattainable for most.

Throughout my short 4 weeks, I found myself loving and hating life all at the same time. I would see how unfair life was for some...how an 8-week-old baby desperately needing a life saving heart surgery would go without this specialized medical care due to a "lack of resources." Knowing in my heart as I kissed the forehead of this small infant, he would soon die in his mother's loving arms.

Who makes the rules?

Who determines life's journeys?

For many here in Afghanistan, they will die quietly and alone in their mud huts...they will be sick, they will be hurt, they will live a life of destitute, and for some...live with no hope. All the while, we continue in our own lives...in our safe corner of our world, never thinking twice about what is taking place in Farah.

I bet for most, you never knew that Farah existed...I know I didn't until now. But now I will know...my family will know, and now you will.

Life is unfair to so many here, and I can become overridden with sadness (if I let it), but I constantly remind myself that I came here for a reason...I came here for a purpose: to make a difference, however small it may be. I know that I did more than just my job here in Farah, and ***I fully understand and witness that not everyone can be saved***.

As I said my goodbyes to the Special Operations Team during my last clinic day, much to everyone's surprise, there was a torrential downpour of rain. The locals said that they had not seen rain like this in years. To me, it was a sign...I chose to walk to the clinic, absorbing every last moment of the surroundings, the mountains, and the coolness of the wet rain as it brushed my cheeks. Once I made it to the front door and walked in for the last time, I took a deep breath and embraced every smell, every sound; I embraced everything about this place...I wanted it to be burned in my memory forever.

When I walked into my clinic room, I opened the glass window panes to hear the beating of the rain hitting the tin that lay on the muddy ground just outside the window. I heard someone call my name, and as I turned around, there stood Zumbida with her mother, Fautha. We embraced with hugs, and I began to tell them goodbye. Our eyes filled with tears, and Fautha handed me a beautiful, soft pink rose that could be smelled from miles away. I could hear the laughter of children and babies' crying...I knew the waiting room was full; I wanted to start seeing patients; after all, it was a race against time for me. I only had two hours before my plane left.

My last patient was a "regular" who was a mother in her early 20's with 4 children. Her youngest son had cerebral palsy and was never going to get better. The woman overheard the interpreter talking about me leaving, and the mother became incredibly sad...she reached out for my hand and asked me to take her son with me. She began to tell me that her family wanted to kill her son because he was too much of a burden. She pleaded over and over to please take him to America...she said, "Please help save his life, please take him, you can make him better."

Inside my mind, I was unraveling at the seams, and I knew there was nothing I could do...I could not control the ending of this poor mother's story, and I was powerless to take her son with me.

I gracefully remind myself that everyone could not be saved, no matter how much I wanted to save this young life...I could not. I hugged the mother and told her how much I would be honored to love and care for her son but that I could not take him with me.

Deep inside, my heart ached for her; I knew that the cold, harsh reality was that this child would inevitably die due to starvation or neglect.

I have had to deal with taking the incredibly good with the unbelievably bad. Knowing that there were some I could save and others that would die. I often would fall asleep at night looking into the black sky under the super bright stars, wondering where God was in all of this. Wondering why all these children who sustained severe burns over their bodies and dying would have to live such a painful, short life...why couldn't they just pass away in their sleep without any pain...then, I soon realized that behind one tragic story, there were thousands more, just like the first. When does it all end for these people, who will be there to help, who will be there to make a difference?

The Farah Experience has been a once in a LIFETIME...a moment in time that can never be redone or duplicated.

For a moment, Farah was magical on every level...I was able to hold the hand of so many women, children, and soldiers who were looking for something to believe in, something to live for.

I was able to hold the bodies of dying and sick children. I was able to put a smile on the faces of many little girls to show them that a woman could be something...a woman could be strong and make a difference in this world.

I was able to be there to care, to provide compassion, to love, to cry, and to listen...I was there to be a part of this Great Farah Experience.

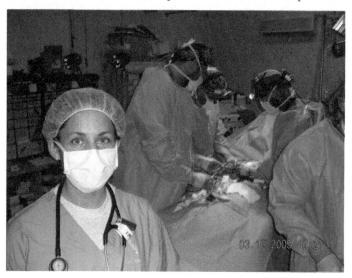

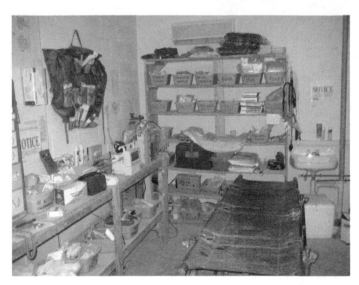

26

THE PRICE OF AFGHAN LIFE

"Too many people today know the price of everything and the
value of nothing."
- Ann Landers

A fghanistan, April 9, 2009

Over the last few days, I have felt overwhelmed.

I am not sure if it has to do with being back at Bagram or if it is
what I have come back to. My first day back seemed relatively simple
and somewhat just the same as I left it. Seeing patients with massive
blast injuries, legs, arms, etc. blown off. The uncertainty if a patient
will live through the night.

However, there was one thing that had changed. We had a unit filled
with small children. I was taken aback by the variety of injuries.

As I received my assignment for the day, most people looked at me
and said, "Good luck; you will be burned out by the end of the shift."
Apparently, this little 8-year-old girl had been here since the 14th of
March and required a lot of attention. For me, this was a good thing.
I didn't see the labor-intensive dressing care or the hourly nursing
interventions that needed to be completed as a negative or a hassle.
What I saw was a small child who would constantly cry out to her
father, "La La, La La."

In her sweet, rugged voice, I saw a child who was injured past the point of recognition. I saw a child who needed to be loved. When I first met Razia, she wouldn't look at anyone, and she clung so tightly to her father's arm. Even though she had been here for a month, she remained frightened of everyone around her, including me. I was determined to change that.

This sweet child, her parents, and her other eight siblings were in their home and found themselves in the middle of a crossfire with the Taliban and Coalition forces. As bullets riddled their home, they hid quietly in rooms to escape the madness that surrounded them. The next thing that would happen would be the defining moment that changed their lives forever.

Their house was hit by a rocket, which blew their home into shreds, killing Razia's two sisters and injuring her mother, father, and a couple of her siblings. Razia's father began to tell me that as he stood up in the middle of what used to be their main room, he watched Razia run to him. Her body was on fire. As he found something to put the fire out, he then put his hand on the back of her head to direct her out of the rubble. He found her skin, hair, and the top of her face and scalp hanging from his hands. He knew that she was gravely injured.

As a parent, I cannot even begin to grasp the concept of seeing one of my own children on fire, much less their face in the palm of my hands. Razia was sent to Bagram from a Forward Operating Base and has been in the TICU for almost a month. She was burned over 40% of her body, and most nurses are burnt out with taking care of her due to the extensive nursing care that is needed to keep her alive and healthy.

When I accepted this assignment, I knew I had come back at the right time. I knew that I could pick up where I left off and continue to make a difference in someone's life. If not in Farah, then in Bagram.

This was my chance. This was my chance to, once again, give my best to love this little girl. To hold her. To sing to her. To give her hugs and kisses like I would my own daughters.

When I looked at Razia, I felt a strong connection with her. I am not sure why; I just did.

After completing my morning assessment and all the paperwork that goes with it, I had a plan. My plan was to get her out of bed and hold her. She had been in the same bed for almost four weeks and needed more than just an every two-hour turn by the nurses. My plan was to take her out of her room, rock her on the rocking chair that sat by the nurse's station, and even give her a ride in a wheelchair.

Sounded simple, right?

It took five people to help get her out of bed and carry her to the nursing station. I held her in my arms for the first time and fell in love with her. I rocked her ever so gently and sang to her. I sang a song that I sang to my girls at home. It's the only song that will stop Reagan from crying when I'm home. For that moment in time, I was her mother. I loved her and held her ever so tight just so that she would know what it felt like to be safe again. She slept soundly, and for the first time, she did not cry out for "La La."

When I looked down into her badly burned face, I could see her peering through the bandages that covered her face, and I caught her smiling at me.

My heart was overjoyed. Even though she was in pain, she loved being rocked, and she loved being held.

The next challenge was to take her for a ride in a wheelchair so that she could see something else other than the four walls in her room. Master Sergeant Rocha brought me a wheelchair and was able to keep her on my lap as he pushed us around the ward meeting new people and saying "hi." At the end of my first day with her she gave me a smile from ear to ear and even a soft quiet laugh.

I knew deep inside of my heart that I did my job, and I did it well that day.

I looked forward to the days ahead so that I could challenge her with new goals in order to get her better.

As the days passed, I was excited to keep little Razia as my patient. On my second day with her, I told her we would get her out of bed and walk for the first time. At first, she insisted that she COULD NOT do it. She did not want to do it.

I told her, "Razia, you can, and you will. I am right here. I will be here to help you and hold you". Reluctantly, she did what I asked, and sure enough, for the first time in over a month, she was walking. There were two people by her side, a person in back of her and a person in front of her. But she did it! She was walking. As she walked for the first time, she began to laugh, almost as if she felt like her "old" self.

As if she was the same little girl before the explosion.

Razia looked at her dad and said, "I am okay. I am walking La La! Look at me! I am okay." I felt like a proud mother. By the end of the week, she became stronger and stronger. She is almost walking on her own, and I am so happy and excited for her.

As our day began to wind down, we had a few visitors. Two members of the military came to meet with her father to discuss Razia's injuries. The two members were here to provide financial compensation for the injuries that the Coalition forces caused.

The father received a hefty sum of Afghan money, but just a small figure in US Dollars when it was calculated out.

I have some mixed emotions about this war, and how we deal with the collateral damage. Meaning the children that get involved in the crossfire of war. As if, somehow, this $127,000 Afghan dollar amount would be able to make everything okay, or better yet, would make a normal life for Razia.

In American dollars, the cost of her life is calculated to be about $2,400.

Razia will need extensive surgeries on her body and face. It won't happen here in Afghanistan. So where will it happen? Who will take care of her once she leaves us? Who will provide plastic surgery to help this little girl's disfigured face so that she can be somewhat normal? How will she live the rest of her life? Who will marry her here in this country?

In this country, she is considered damaged goods. As if the sum of money that was given to her father would "fix" the fact that this child has NO future here. Not only did Razia's family receive monetary compensation, but two other children's families received money today. The only thing that processed through my mind was. "So, this is the going rate for an Afghan child?"

I was sick to my stomach.

I began to sweat. I wanted to cry.

As Razia's father accepted the money, I just looked at Razia. I looked at her little hands that would reach out for my face when I was near, and then right at the moment when I wanted to scream at the top of my lungs, she began to wave at me for the first time. All my frustration inside melted away. I went to her side and just held her hand and smiled at her.

When I think about this country and the children who are here in our TICU, I think about their futures here. If we were in America, it wouldn't be an issue. These children would live a pretty normal life. People in the states are accepting, and these children would be able to recover from their traumatic injuries. However, we are not in America. We are in Afghanistan, and the alternative to these severe injuries is death. Never in my life would I have ever thought that letting a child die would be better than saving them. These children who are saved with life-changing injuries will now live a life that may be more tragic and painful than death.

They will be considered a burden to their families. They will be neglected. They will eventually starve to death or be killed. Afghanistan is not set up for long-term care or even rehabilitation. Most people are so poor they can't, or won't, keep up with the medical needs of these innocent children.

It is a constant internal struggle. I see my 8-year-old child who was burned, a 3-year-old girl who lost her left arm due to being run over by a Humvee, and a 5-year-old child who was hit in the head with a rocket-propelled grenade (RPG) and died once in the operating room, but we brought her back. She was saved for what? She is now paralyzed on the right side; she cannot talk, and she is completely incontinent of stool and urine. These children will never be the same, and it is unknown how their families will deal with what the war has given them.

My first week back at Bagram has been a roller coaster of emotions. The feelings of laughter, sorrow, pain, and accomplishment have filled the air. The reality of life here is harsh and unforgiving. The story is not closed yet.

Razia will be with me for a while. I hope I can continue to care for her, love her like she was my own child, and see how she grows and becomes more "normal" every day.

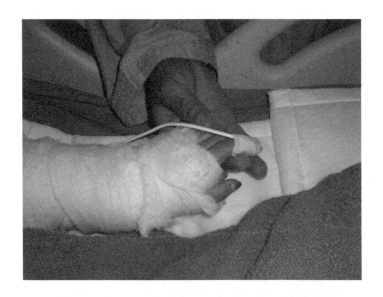

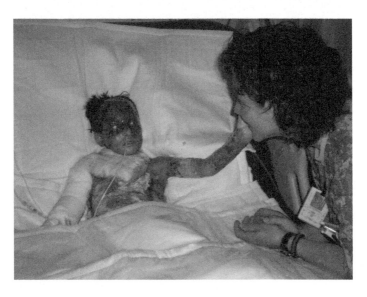

27

— · —

STRENGTH AND FORTITUDE

"In wartime, truth is so precious that she should always be
attended by a bodyguard of lies."
— Prime Minister Winston Churchill

M y patient, my 4th daughter, Razia, made international news.
"June 2009: BAGRAM AIR BASE, Afghanistan -
The American military doctors watched in horror as the oxygen mask
on the young Afghan girl's face started to melt.

The 8-year-old's skin was smoking from white phosphorus, a lethal
chemical. Her hair was burned away. Her face, head, neck and arms
were scorched yellow, pink and black. When the doctors tried to scrape
away the dead tissue, flames leapt out."

Next came a piece from the Associated Press after she'd recovered.

Afghan girl burned by white phosphorus heads home
By RAHIM FAIEZ - Associated Press Writer
BAGRAM AIR BASE, Afghanistan - The nurse fixed the black wig
on Razia's scarred and disfigured scalp before the 8-year-old took off
around the emergency room to bid farewell to the staff who cared for her
after white phosphorus scorched her face, head, neck, and hands. When
Razia came to the US military hospital four months ago, Cpt. Christine
Collins didn't think she would make it out alive. On Wednesday, the

little Afghan girl left this military hospital for an arduous journey to her little village, a 50 mile drive from Bagram Air Base...It's unclear where the white phosphorus came from that disfigured Razia for life - burning her face now marked with permanent scars.

... White phosphorus Burns until it's gone. And with Burns over 40 to 45% of her body, few thought Razia would survive when she first airlifted to the US hospital. "This is kind of a dream come true for everybody, for her to be able to go home," Collins said, while choking back her tears. It was a long journey for both her and I. She is like my fourth daughter,: she said.

Collins, a military nurse from Miami, Arizona and a mother of three girls back in the US was the first to care for Razia, and she slowly coaxed a smile, and then a step, and finally a recovery from her - over 4 months and 15 shirt surgeries. She will be coming back again for treatment at the hospital in Bagram after a couple of weeks, and then also continue with therapy on hospital in Kabul.

But the scars are there for all to see in the hospital staff quietly worries that Razia may never have a normal life in Afghanistan, where women in the countryside are mostly defined by the marriage they enter.

"I will always wonder and think about her for the rest of my life," Collins said."

I'm a nurse. I'm not a munitions expert and I certainly don't understand chemistry the way a PhD does, but what I have seen is white phosphorous used on humans. Specifically, Razia.

At its basis, white phosphorus munitions are a type of incendiary weapon that uses white phosphorus to produce intense heat and smoke. These munitions are used for several purposes: they can create smoke screens to hide troop movements, mark targets, or light up an area. When white phosphorus burns, it produces a thick white smoke and can burn intensely enough to ignite fabrics, fuel, ammunition, and other combustibles.

Due to its ability to cause severe burns and injuries, the use of white phosphorus is highly controversial, especially in civilian-populated areas. There are international regulations governing its use under certain conditions, particularly in terms of its effects on civilians during armed conflicts.

Controversial? To say the least. To this day, I don't think any government took responsibility for the use of it that day. And to be truthful, who knows how often it was weaponized against the enemy or even innocent civilians.

This is just one of the many truly misunderstood parts of war.

Yes, war is ugly.

Yes, people die.

And yes, the news reports shower the airwaves and papers. But it is never the same on TV or in the papers as in real life.

A newscast or article can't transmit the agony, the pain, the suffering, the look between the eyes of a nurse and a patient who she knows is about to take his last breath, and all that goes through their minds is a final thought that dies with us.

Razia showed me strength and fortitude like no other patient. It was different, and I think it was different because of her innocence.

28

— . —

THE CRIES OF A CHILD

"In the end, we are all just children, searching for love and validation."
- Craig DiLouie, Suffer The Children

A fghanistan, April 20, 2009

When a child cries it's almost instinct that a mother would love and hold her child to sooth away their pain, sorrow, and tears.

The bond between a mother and a child is never-ending. The love is everlasting and endures through all times. It is when a mother looks into her newborn's eyes, and in that one instant, that one split second, she knows her life has forever changed. The life that she once knew would never be the same. How her life would change, she would not know, but deep in the corner of her heart she recognizes that her child's dreams would NOW be her dreams. The good that she once wanted for herself would NOW be the good for her child. The feelings of being loved, the joy of the warm sun on her face would now be the wishes and the wants for her own child. A mother would now know such a deep love that would be overwhelming and confusing all in the same.

Such a profound and enduring love for a human being that she has never in her life experienced before. It is the love of her child that now she would give her own life for.

I would give my own life for my children. I would walk through fire for them. I would take every difficult day for them. The love I hold for my three daughters runs deeper than the bluest ocean. My love is free flowing with no strings attached. The love a mother has for her children is irreplaceable and unbreakable. I would give anything for my children.

To always and forever be with them.

To kiss them goodnight, to hold their sweet little hands when we are walking down a busy street, to smell their hair at the end of a long play day.

To see my beautiful Kennedy look at me with her brownish-green eyes and hear her tell me that she loves me.

To play with Taylor in a makeshift fort that we build in her room and read stories with a flashlight while Reagan cries.

To see Reagan hold so tightly to her daddy's shirt, all the while watching her peer at me through her long bangs which cover her eyes.

To see her sneak a smile at me and then hide her face in her daddy's arm.

What mother wouldn't want to love their child? To hold them, to keep them safe, to keep them from harm's way?

My little Razia is doing better. Her father left last week to help the family recover from the tragic bombing that destroyed their home. He is finding a place for Razia's mother and other siblings to live. Since his departure, Razia has been withdrawn and refuses to eat. I have tried everything. Even a full ice cream diet at one point. I am doing my best for her. I made a promise to her father that I would take care of her and keep her safe.

Today was a tough day for her. She was terribly upset and was crying to the point where she was inconsolable. Using an interpreter, I soon realized Razia was not in pain, she was not hungry, and her diaper did not need to be changed.

Razia wanted her mother. She cried and cried to hear her mother's voice. I immediately took the phone and began to try contacting her with no luck.

Finally, after three hours, we were able to reach her father. He said that Razia's mother could not get to the phone. I then told her father that it was important that Razia speak to her mother, and she needed to come visit Razia.

Unfortunately, from what I understood from the father, Razia's mother will not be coming. She will not be here to hold or love Razia. To tell Razia that everything will be okay when she's scared or needs her mother's loving arms around her. It's too difficult for Razia's mother to see her burnt and disfigured. Razia's mom cannot bear to see her like "this".

I sat next to Razia's bedside, while Razia's uncle explained that her mother would not be on the telephone and would be returning with her father next week.

Little Razia sobbed for her mother and cried out repeatedly. As the tears began to pour down her delicate, burnt face, I found myself crying. There was nothing I could do. I could not hold her enough, I could not love her enough, and I could not soothe her broken heart.

She wanted her own mother. The mother that used to love her. The mother that once cared for her. The mother whose love should be never ending, and that would go to the ends of the earth for her. To be by her side, to hold her, to make everything okay.

As Razia cried harder and harder, I let her scream and kick. I felt so helpless. My heart ached for her, and then my heart began to ache for my own children.

As I held little Razia, the cries of a child will be etched in my mind and heart forever. The look on her face, the hurt in her eyes, the feeling of rejection that was exuding from her soft brown eyes. All I could do was hold her. I didn't think it was enough. I know it wasn't enough for her, but she soon cried herself to sleep. During this moment as I began to rock her and sing to her, my mind drifted. I thought of my own children.

I began to think of the many times they have cried for me since I have been gone. For their own mom to hold them, to love them, to make everything okay. I began to think about the many times they had fallen and needed a hug from mommy... but I too was not there.

I often wonder what will be the ultimate price that I will have to pay once my deployment is finished. Will Taylor understand where I have been and what I have been doing? This weighs heavy on my heart because it is so painful when she asks me, *"Mommy, do you have one more little girl to take care of, and then you come home for me?"*

Will my children know how much I have loved them and how I thought about them every day that passed?

Will my children know that I have loved them enough?

Will they know that I will never abandon them?

Will they know that I carried them in my heart every step of the way during this fucked up journey?

Will they know that it is because of them, and their father that kept me going and encouraged me to fully open my heart and love the children of Afghanistan? These children would know their names and know who they are.

They would know Kennedy, Taylor, and Reagan. They would hear their names in the same songs I would sing to them as babies. Somehow, these same songs would now soothe the cries of an Afghan child. I will continue to hold and love these children.

I will give them comfort for their most difficult days and provide them with faith so that they can believe, have hope, and grow stronger every day.

Taylor Collins, 4 yrs old with Dusty. Photo taken a few days after Collins deployed

29

SLOOP JOHN B

"So hoist up the John B's sail,
See how the main sail sets,
Call for the captain ashore,
Let me go home,
Let me go home
I wanna go home, yeah, yeah
Well, I feel so broke up
I wanna go home"
– The Beach Boys

Afghanistan, April 29, 2009

Today was an especially strange day.

At first, it started off just like any other day. Patients with IED blasts to the face, arms, and legs. Patients on life support. Patients with traumatic brain injuries. Patients who were inevitably going to die. As the day began to fly by, we were informed that we were going to receive two, possibly three, new admissions to the TICU.

As always, the charge nurse begins to crunch the number of patients to the amount of nurses we have available. At the same time, the head physician comes running through the TICU doors; he begins to yell..."Get bed 8 and bed 13 to the floor NOW; we have three inbound!"

As the charge nurse broke out the new assignments, me, Lt Jackson, and Lt Wilson were ready for our new admissions. But what was so different about these admissions, they were not your typical "adult" TICU patients.

They were small children.

The first admission rolls through the door. Not only was I shocked, but the rest of the nursing staff was shocked. This was an almost 5-pound, one-day-old baby boy who was diagnosed with a birth defect and needed surgical intervention. The baby's abdominal contents were formed on the outside of his stomach as the stomach closed in utero. Our team of physicians had decided to provide humanitarian assistance to this baby's family and repair his birth defect. Lt. Olivia Jackson was assigned this small baby. She was a great nurse and would be able to quickly adapt to anything that was thrown her way.

Within a few minutes, our next two patients came to the TICU.

Both patients were intubated and on life support. These two patients were 5 and 10 years old. We all were shocked to see such traumatic injuries to these boys. As we began to get the boys settled, we began to ask questions as to how the boys were injured. When we discovered the story of the events that took place, I could not believe it.

Here in Afghanistan, you've been raised in a country that knows nothing else but war. You have lived for decades amid war, and there are constant reminders, such as buildings that have never been rebuilt due to continuous bombings. The war is always around you and where you live. Not only is there rubble that surrounds your everyday existence, but there are also signs that are posted everywhere saying, "Danger: Landmines." This includes the rusted-out armored vehicles that lay scattered across the land of Afghanistan from when the Russians invaded over 20 years ago.

Here, in this country, there are always reminders every day and everywhere that this country is torn by the many wars it has faced and continues to face today.

So this leads me to my disbelief and overwhelming feeling of discontent.

Today, as a group of boys played in their small village just outside of Kabul, they found an old landmine and began to play with it. Now, unbelievably, this is a regular occurrence in this country for children to come across such deadly and volatile objects.

Most children will carefully collect the landmines and sell them to the local Taliban for a small price so that their families may eat for another day. Others will jab at the landmines or throw rocks at them, trying to set it off.

Well, today this group of children decided to be "boys" and throw rocks at the landmine they had discovered. As each rock was thrown, it got closer and closer to the trigger mechanism, and finally, on the last rock thrown, hit the trigger in just the right place and detonated the landmine.

The denotation spared no life in its path.

It knew no difference between an innocent child, a man, or a woman. This landmine took the lives of two small children and critically injured three others. One of the three boys was admitted to the Egyptian hospital for treatment, and the other two were sent to our TICU.

Lt. Wilson was assigned to the 5-year-old with the deadly sucking chest wound and open belly due to the amount of shrapnel that penetrated this young boy's chest and body. My 10-year-old boy's mouth and lower jaw were blasted open by the debris and rocks that flew through the air and embedded into his trachea. He, too, had multiple chest tubes placed due to his right lung collapsing.

As we settled our new arrivals, I just couldn't get over the way these injuries occurred. I know, back home, I worry about my girls riding their bikes or climbing too high in our backyard tree. I worry about how high they swing on the swing or when Kennedy walks to the convenience store. As a mother, I worry about my children, their well-being, and their safety. I worry because I love them, and I want them to forever be out of harm's way.

Never in my life would I know such a worry as a mother in Afghanistan. Their worries and cries are often unheard. Children are lost every day to this type of tragic event. I could only imagine the "uproar" that something like this would cause if it happened in the United States.

IT WOULDN'T HAPPEN!

WE WOULD NOT ALLOW IT TO HAPPEN!

There would be support organizations, human rights activists, and volunteer support to create a safe community for our children. There would be no rock unturned in America if one of our own children were killed or severely injured due to a landmine found in our backyard or at a local park.

Being here, being one person, sometimes I feel helpless. I give and give to this place and many days I go "*home*" feeling so empty and sad. There have been many days that I just can't write. My mind is overworked, my heart is empty, and I am filled with such a deep and empty sadness over the many things that I have endured and experienced here. I constantly remind myself of the once bright light that I carried when I first arrived in Afghanistan.

I count on that light.

It's the light at the end of a long tunnel that will still be there when I return home. My once bright eyes will not be dimmed. They will continue to shine. I will dig deep within myself to persevere, to continue to give the children of Afghanistan hope, give them love, provide support, and encourage them to be "somebody" when they grow-up. To make an impact on their world and on their country.

This life experience is truly a blessing.

As the music played in the background, "Sloop John B" by The Beach Boys, my mind could hear nothing else but the lyric of "Well I feel so broke up, I want to go home I want to go home, let me go."

As my eyes began to water, I took a big sigh and looked around my now-transformed trauma ICU, which had been converted into a full-blown PICU (Pediatric Intensive Care Unit).

It was one of those time-stopping moments; when I looked at each child's bedside, I saw each nurse steadfast to their little patient, holding the child's hand, caressing their small faces, and singing the same song that I was singing...

"I wanna go home."

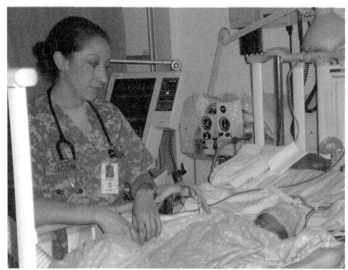

1st Lt Olivia Jackson

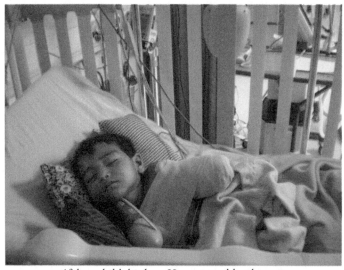

Afghan child, hit by a Humvee and lost her arm

30

— • —

FARAH PART 2

"An eye for an eye only ends up making the whole world blind."
— Mahatma Gandhi

The Associated Press: May 6, 2009

Red Cross: Many Afghans dead after U.S. bombings

KABUL — The international Red Cross confirmed "dozens of bodies" on Wednesday in graves and rubble where Afghan officials alleged U.S. bombs killed civilians, and the Afghan president said his first meeting with President Barack Obama would focus on the issue.

The International Committee of the Red Cross reported Wednesday its officials saw women and children among dozens of bodies in two villages targeted by airstrikes, while the U.S. military sent a brigadier general to the region to investigate.

A former Afghan government official said up to 120 people died in the bombing Monday evening. The first images from the bombings in Farah province emerged Wednesday. Photos from the site obtained by The Associated Press showed villagers burying the dead in about a dozen fresh graves, while others dug through the rubble of demolished mud-brick homes.

A team from the international Red Cross traveled to Bala Baluk district in Farah on Tuesday, where the officials saw "dozens of bodies in each of the two locations that we went to," said spokeswoman Jessica Barry.

"There were bodies, there were graves, and there were people burying bodies when we were there," she said. "We do confirm women and children. There were women and children." Karzai ordered a probe Wednesday into the killings and the U.S. military sent a brigadier general to Farah to head a U.S. investigation, said Col. Greg Julian, a U.S. spokesman. Afghan military and police officials were also part of the investigative team...

...Karzai called civilian casualties "unacceptable."

Civilian deaths have caused increasing friction between the Afghan and U.S. governments, and Karzai has long pleaded with American officials to reduce the number of civilian casualties in their operations. U.S. and NATO officials accuse the Taliban militants of fighting from within civilian homes, thus putting them in danger.

Mohammad Nieem Qadderdan, a former district chief of Bala Buluk, said between 100 and 120 people were killed in the attacks. He said villagers were still uncovering bodies, some of which were missing limbs or were torn into small pieces, he said.

"People are still looking through the rubble," Qadderdan said. "We need more people to help us. Many families left the villages, fearing other strikes." Provincial authorities have told villagers not to bury the bodies, but instead to line them up for the officials conducting the investigation to see, Qadderdan said.

The fighting broke out Monday soon after Taliban fighters — including Taliban from Pakistan and Iran — massed in Farah province in western Afghanistan, said Belqis Roshan, a member of Farah's provincial council. The provincial police chief, Abdul Ghafar, said 25 militants and three police officers died in that battle near the village of

Ganjabad in Bala Baluk district, a Taliban-controlled area near the border with Iran.

Villagers told Afghan officials they put children, women, and elderly men in several housing compounds in the village of Gerani — about 3 miles (4.8 kilometers) to the east — to keep them safe. But villagers said fighter aircraft later targeted those compounds, killing a majority of those inside, according to Roshan and other officials.

A Western official in Kabul said Marine special operations forces — which fall under the U.S. coalition — called in the airstrikes. The official asked not to be identified because he wasn't authorized to release the information.

Villagers brought about 30 bodies, including women and children, to Farah city to show the governor Tuesday, said Abdul Basir Khan, a member of the provincial council.

Journalists and human rights workers can rarely visit remote battle sites to verify claims of civilian casualties. U.S. officials say Taliban militants sometimes force villagers to lie and say civilians have died in coalition strikes. But the international Red Cross report and other official accounts added weight to villagers' claims in Bala Baluk.

In remarks in the United States on Tuesday, Karzai alluded to the problem of civilian casualties without mentioning the bombing deaths. He said the success of the new U.S. war strategy depends on "making sure absolutely that Afghans don't suffer — that Afghan civilians are protected."

"This war against terrorism will succeed only if we fight it from a higher platform of morality," he said in a speech at the Brookings Institution in Washington. Asked later to clarify, Karzai said, "We must be conducting this war as better human beings," and recognize that "force won't buy you obedience."

*An Afghan government commission previously found that an Au-
gust 2008 operation by U.S. forces killed 90 civilians in Azizabad, a
finding backed by the U.N. The U.S. originally said no civilians died;
a high-level investigation later concluded 33 civilians were killed. After
the Azizabad killings, the top U.S. commander in Afghanistan, Gen.
David McKiernan, announced a directive last September meant to
reduce such deaths. He ordered commanders to consider breaking away
from a firefight in populated areas rather than pursue militants into
villages.*

*Associated Press reporters Heidi Vogt, Jason Straziuso, and Fisnik
Abrashi contributed to this report from Kabul.*

Death.

So much death.

And I was there.

This is where I was, with this nimble, ready-to-save, Army Forward
Surgical Team. It pains me to read this article. It's not what I saw. It's
not what I experienced.

Don't get me wrong, there was war, and there was death, and there
was poverty to the likes that I've never seen, but to them, it was simply
called life.

I don't think I have anything more to say on that except...

Dissonance.

That one word jumps out at me in a profound and deep way. The
stark, clinical language of casualty counts and political statements feels
so far removed from the Farah I knew, the Farah that lives on in my
heart.

It's not that I'm naive to the realities of war, to the inevitable
collateral damage and the heartbreaking loss of innocent lives. I saw
those realities up close, in the broken bodies and shattered lives that
passed through our field hospital. I felt the weight of those impossible

choices, the ones that haunt you long after the dust has settled and the world has moved on.

But I also saw something else in Farah, something that the news reports and the official statements so often miss. I saw resilience, compassion, and a fierce, unshakeable hope in the face of unimaginable adversity. I saw it in the eyes of the mothers who brought their sick children to our clinic and in the smiles of the little girls who dared to dream of a different future. I saw it in the unwavering dedication of my Army brothers, in the way we lifted each other up and found a sliver of beauty in the ugliest of times.

That's the Farah I choose to remember. That's the Farah that changed me, not just as a nurse or a service member, but as a human being.

And I think, in a way, that's the lesson I want to share with you.

In a world that so often feels defined by tragedy and conflict, by the heartbreaking headlines and the endless cycle of suffering, it's easy to lose sight of the small, precious moments of grace.

The moments of connection, of shared humanity, of love in the face of all that would seek to destroy it. Don't lose sight of those moments... it can be the difference between life and death.

31

— • —

Don't Quit

...Tired is my body
...Tired is my mind
...Tired is my soul
and
...Tired is my heart.
- Andlib Farid

Afghanistan: May 22, 2009

It is now the end of May, and this month has been a difficult one for me.

This month marks many life changes and memories for me. Looking back on the weeks that have passed seems like I have just closed my eyes and walked through each day like I didn't exist. As if I turned into a machine getting through the day. Unemotional, unphased by the tragedy. As if no one was home, the lights are off, and I'm on autopilot. I still can't believe there are only 8 days left in this month, and it's over.

I think my mode of being on autopilot reflects my unwillingness to accept not being with my family to celebrate our personal and professional successes. Today, May 22" is our wedding anniversary. May 20th marked my promotion to Captain; how I would dream of my promotion ceremony, seeing my girls and Clinton there, letting the girls and Clinton pin my Captain bars on my collar. Maybe next time.

May 11th marked my graduation from the Air Force's professional military education course at Squadron Officer School. May 29th is my Nana's wedding anniversary, not to mention my own parents and my aunts and uncles. And then there is May 31st, Clinton's birthday.

A year ago today, I wondered where we would be and what we would be doing. What our plans would be. Where would we go for dinner? How Clinton and I would laugh at another year gone by, and we would comment that we are still in love, just like the day we met. Then, we would take a moment, look at our lives, and acknowledge all the changes, good and bad. The chaotic life with our three dramatic daughters and smile. We would know that we would not want to be anywhere else but here...with each other, with our girls, and the crazy life that we built – loving one another.

Let us not forget this month also marks my fifth month downrange. At times, I wished I could lay my head on my pillow and not wake-up until the first week of July. Just thinking about leaving this place, I get a surge of emotions that will almost take over my heart and mind. That is, if I let it. I can now feel the struggle of making it another 6 weeks.

I am tired.

I am sad.

I am tired of putting up with the "deployment life."

I am tired of worrying, of caring, of loving.

I want to go to a quiet place and just "BE."

I want to be left alone.

I don't want to hear anyone crying, and

I don't want anyone telling me "dar," which means pain.

I don't want to hear Razia crying out for "Lala."

I don't want to see the children hurt in the crossfires of war.

I don't want to see any more blood-soaked or stained beds and floors.

I don't want to see any more dead bodies, blown off arms, legs, faces.

I don't want any of this anymore.

I don't want to tell any more soldiers that they made it, but their friend did not.

I don't want to tell any more soldiers that they've lost their legs, or that they are paralyzed for life, or that they have lost their vision.

I don't want to be the strong one anymore.

I don't want to pretend I'm the tough one.

I don't want to be the one with all the answers.

I don't want to see families torn apart and lives changed forever.

Just a few days ago, we had a bay full of American soldiers. They were all involved in an explosion just outside our base. And three days ago, one of our female logistic lieutenants was killed by a roadside bomb coming from Kabul.

After 5 months of this, I am tired. I am tired of seeing the devastating effects of war. At times, I feel like my compassion has lessened or my sympathy is dwindling. I can't believe that I am even writing this, but this is how I feel at this exact moment.

It's the raw truth: the hurt that fills my heart and what my eyes can never unsee.

This is my reality.

I can remember when I first got here, and I was writing and writing. I have taken some time to try and figure out why I've stopped. Is it because it's too hard? Or is it my way of just dealing with what's going on right now? Or even worse, is it because I have become used to this crazy, fucked-up world here.

This crazy life, which is *my life* right now? Have I just come to accept this life and expect what I see on an everyday basis? At times I feel as if my emotions have run dry or they have been temporarily paused.

We received a 12-month-old baby last week. He came in with burns to his buttocks, legs, and testicles. The family stated that the little baby grabbed a pot of boiling water and "accidentally" splashed the boiling water over his body, causing his burns.

After further examination, it was evident that this injury was no accident.

The burns were indicative of a "dipping" injury which is not an accident. It's a form of child abuse. This poor baby was dipped in boiling water as a way of punishment. This was child abuse, and guess what? After we finish taking care of him, grafting his burns, and making him "normal" or as normal as he could possibly be, he will go home to the same family that abused him. How can I accept this? How can anyone accept this?

Inside, I am screaming at the top of my lungs. This is madness for me. It has been too difficult to accept at times.

When he cries, I will hold and cuddle him. I will sing him to sleep, but I will not be his nurse. When I first got here, I would have picked him for a patient. I just cannot. It is too hard. When I hear him cry, I just want to scoop him up in my arms and take him home. But it is not possible, and I wonder what will happen to him after he goes home. Not to mention what will happen to all the other children we have saved and cared for.

There is so much that I do not want to do anymore.

I am tired.

I feel finished inside.

But in the midst of the craziness of my so-called life here, I must remind myself that what I do now...what I do for the next 6 weeks is what matters the most. This moment, during this time, will be my moment of grace. Being able to make the choice to preserve, knowing I must finish even if it seems impossible.

I must finish.

Giving it my all, one last time, to preserve. This is what will define me. A transformation will occur from an ordinary person to an extraordinary woman which will lead me to do extraordinary things. Life changing things.

Now, more than ever, I must persevere. I need to remain steadfast. I need to continue to give my best and not give up. Even though there have been many days that I wanted to, I can feel myself building a wall. I can feel myself detaching and deflecting all the bad that continues to come, trying my best to shelter myself.

When I first entered the Air Force in 1994 and arrived at Peterson AFB, there was a TSgt who was providing a "new" airmen's in-processing brief. This TSgt gave every one of us a card with a poem attached to the back of it. I have kept this poem in my wallet all these years, and when I don't think I can make it or when I feel like I have nothing else to give, I read this poem to myself and re-read it again and again. In some straightforward way, it makes a difference to me, and maybe in some small way, it will you, too.

Don't Quit

When things go wrong, as they sometimes will,
When the road you're trudging seems all uphill,
When the funds are low, and the debts are high,
And you want to smile, but you have to sigh.
When care is pressing you down a bit,
Rest if you must, but don't you quit.

Life is strange with its twists and turns,
As every one of us sometimes learns,
And many a failure comes about,
When he might have won if he'd stuck it out,
Don't give up though the pace seems slow,
You might succeed with another blow.
Success is failure turned inside out,
The silver tint of the clouds of doubt,
And you never can tell how close you are,
It may be near when it seems so far,
So stick to the fight when you're hardest hit,
It's when things seem worst that you must not quit.

What is the meaning of perseverance to me?

Never quitting.

Being steadfast.

A state of mind.

Determination.

A defining moment.

Never giving up.

Continue to move forward, even if one must take a step back.

TO KEEP MOVING FORWARD.

I have and will continue to stick it out, and I will not quit!

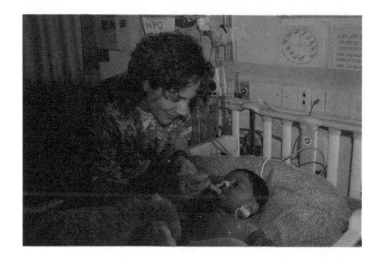

32

—•—

WONDER TWINS ACTIVATE

"Be strong, be fearless, be beautiful. And believe that anything is possible when you have the right people there to support you."
— Misty Copeland, American ballet dancer

A fghanistan, May 25, 2009

To have complete trust in one person is a lot to give up, especially when they are not a spouse, a close relative, or even a best friend for whom you have known since childhood.

Having someone you can trust and rely on, who will always do right by you and support the responsibilities you are charged with, is invaluable. Knowing that this person, here in Afghanistan, has your back 100% and you have hers creates a bond that is both rare and astonishing. Together, you face challenges and overcome obstacles, knowing that nothing can bring you down. For me, that person for me is *Lt. Olivia Jackson*.

Last night, the overhead paging system in the hospital rang out, "Level 1 trauma in the ER, Level 1 trauma in the ER." I quickly left the ICU to respond to the trauma. As I got there, I gowned and gloved up; we were waiting for a man in his 20s to arrive at any moment that had been crushed between two large up-armored vehicles. As the outer doors of the trauma bay opened and the medics rolled in with all their gear, this young Afghan male presented with a large external fixator that held his right humerus together, and his abdomen was completely open with bowl content sliding under the makeshift dressing that was once secured by tape.

This patient was bleeding from his nose, ears, abdomen, right arm, and chest. He had two chest tubes in place and was on life support. From the first appearance of this man, he looked like he was not going to make it. As our trauma team gathered around the patient to do what we know best, saving lives, everything began to fall into place. The ER physician completed her primary assessment and then we moved to the secondary assessment. The head physician was calling for another chest tube set-up.

We had to move quickly! This person's life depended on it.

As all the physicians peered over the patient and began the appropriate interventions, the new trauma czar (leader) asked for Mannitol. When this patient was first injured at a Forward Operating Base, the medical team had infused over 19 units of packed red blood cells, 7 units of fresh frozen plasma, 5 units of whole blood, and 1 unit of cryoprecipitate. Needless to say, he received a lot of blood products. Probably a little more than he needed, and now the physicians were worried about cerebral edema. So, in order to protect his brain, we gave him the mannitol IV push. As the 3rd chest tube was placed, we quickly rushed the patient to the CT scanner. During the transport, the patient began to be increasingly unstable and presented with cardiac dysrhythmias.

The physicians began to yell out orders to give 1 gram of magnesium, 2 amps of calcium, 10 of vecuronium, and 100 mcg of Fentanyl. All IV push NOW! I said, "Yes Sir!" as I looked at the exit doors, there she stood, Lt. Olivia Jackson, my partner in crime, my person, the other half of me since being here in Afghanistan.

Right when Olivia saw my face, she knew I needed something. She went right by my side and said, "What can I do to help?" I just smiled and told her, "You always know when to show up!" Olivia laughed and said she could hear me calling her in her mind and rushed right over to the CT room. As I listed the items we needed, we split them up in two so that we could get what we needed in half the time.

Within minutes, both of us were back at the CT room with all the medications waiting to enter. Once the scan was completed and it was safe to go to the patient, Olivia carefully but quickly handed me the drugs, and I pushed each ordered drug. The patient was very unstable and needed to get to the OR as soon as possible. Olivia never left my side. There she was ready to help in any way possible. To be there for an extra set of eyes, to be a runner, to do whatever was needed to save this person's life.

When we work together, something magical happens. It is like a synergistic effect. We are on top of our game. We both know what each other is thinking, and we are always right there by one another's side. We are a part of a talented team, and we have experienced something wonderful together. Saving lives! I think we are such a well-oiled machine because we have been by each other's side since the first day of our deployment and have been through many codes, deaths, and life-saving situations. This is why we work well together.

In any given situation, she is either doing chest compressions, or I am pushing drugs, or she is running like she is in the Belmont Stakes, rapidly infusing over 44 units of blood products into a dying patient while I am doing chest compressions. I cannot begin to say how much I love and appreciate her for what she does for me and the team.

After the CT was over and we transferred the patient to the OR, there Olivia was. Sitting at the nurses' station, asking how the patient was doing. I simply told her, "I don't think it looks good." She just smiled and said, "We did the best we could for him. We'll just wait to see what happens next." Within an hour and a half, the patient was now being admitted to our TICU. He would be my patient. This guy had so much going on. Too much to wrap your head around.

He had drains coming from his face and mouth, multiple chest tubes, an open abdomen that was to wall suction, and a right humerus fracture with a large external fixator in place. Multiple rib fractures, he had a cordis in the left groin, multiple peripheral IV sites, and a left subclavian triple-lumen catheter.

Now, he also needed all his drugs to be started. I am talking about several. A Fentanyl drip, Propofol drip, Lasix drip, dobutamine drip, and Normal Saline IV fluids. Not to mention multiple antibiotics, and we were now starting a bedside bronchoscopy.

The whole situation could have been overwhelming if I allowed it. But it was so exhilarating for me. To work under pressure like that gives me a high that can last for days. There was so much to do in so little time (LESS THAN 2 hours). Once again, there was Olivia. Steadfast by my side. With one look at each other, we knew we could "rock-n-roll" this patient! With music in the air and a high five, we were ready to go.

And it was GO TIME for us!

When situations like this present themselves, they remind me of an old cartoon my brother and I would watch as kids and would act out the cartoon characters throughout the house.

"The Wonder Twins".

Tonight was a perfect example of the Wonder Twins for Olivia and me. I felt so alive tonight, more alive than I have felt in a long time. Tonight re-awoke my fire. My resilience as a nurse.

I was excited.

I was happy.

I was glad to be here.

I was happy to have Olivia at my side, doing this shit together. She has been my saving grace, and I have been hers.

Olivia has been like a sister to me; I wholeheartedly trust her, and I am so thankful that she was placed with me at this time, this moment, to do the things we are doing together. I wouldn't have wanted to do any of this without her. We are truly teammates here. We both know when we need a hug, when we need help, or when we need an ear to listen.

Olivia, thank you for being you.

Thank you for being such a wonderful and caring nurse.

Thank you for always being there for me.

Thank you for always having my back.

I could not have been half the nurse here in Afghanistan without you. In the end, our patient is now stable. He will need to go back to the OR for additional surgeries. He is stable and just might make it to live another day. We have such a wonderful trauma team. I am grateful to have been a part of something so amazing and life-changing.

1st Lt Olivia Jackson and Capt Christine Collins

Capt Christine Collins and "The" 1st Lt Olivia Jackson. "Wonder
Twins Power Activate"

33

— . —

FALLEN COMRADE CEREMONY

"So long as they speak your name, you shall never die."
—— **Dan Brown, American author**

A fghanistan, May 26, 2009

As the sun began to set on the Afghan mountain, the red, orange, and yellow colors blazed across the sky like a fire.

The time was 1800 hours, and everyone across the base could hear the voice on the loudspeaker, "Attention all personnel, there will be a fallen comrade ceremony at 1830. All available personnel will report to Disney Drive."

As I was leaving the hospital, I could hear the "giant voice" and quickly ran to my room and changed into the proper uniform to report to Disney Drive, which is the main street on base. I walked with a friend and talked about how beautiful the evening was. As we walked and talked, all I could think about was the Air Force members who just died. My mind began to drift as to how they died, and wondered if their families already knew. These two service members died in an IED explosion. At the time of the explosion, there was an additional trailing vehicle that felt the impact of the blast and stopped their vehicle right in its tracks. The surviving Air Force members who were in the trailing vehicle ran to the aid of the fiery mess. The person who had been driving the vehicle that hit the IED was still alive and screaming as she burned alive. The members could not get to her, and she died.

Back at home, before I got here and heard about soldiers dying from bombs, IED blasts, gunfire, etc., I was ignorant to assume that all these soldiers were conducting some type of "covert mission" or that they were low crawling through minefields in support of a covert mission, or that their death was immediate and most likely didn't feel the pain of death.

Don't get me wrong; there are highly elite soldiers that conduct these types of dangerous missions on the daily. But what I am talking about is the instant harm that comes to each soldier being here. The "average" ones. The soldiers who are doing their normal daily activities. The ones that drive from Bagram to Kabul weekly, or other soldiers that provide security because they are "security forces," "infantry," or even a "logistics troop," and it is their "turn" to leave the wire.

As all these thoughts ran through my mind, I got closer to the place where I would stand to pay my last respects to my fellow Air Force comrades.

As we got in line, I could see the sun peeking out from the clouds that covered the sky. The wind began to pick up, and I could feel the dirt sticking to the Chapstick that covered my lips. As I rubbed my lips together, it felt like sandpaper. Everything was quiet. I could hear my own heart beating in my chest. As I looked to my left and looked to my right, all I could see was hundreds and hundreds of soldiers who lined Disney Drive. The entire base was closed for business. Unfortunately, this type of ceremony has become a common occurrence.

I quickly stood at attention and rendered a salute to the vehicles that were slowly driving by. There were two large trucks, and each vehicle carried a casket draped with an American flag. Each vehicle carried members of the dead soldier's unit. While the vehicles passed,

I could see the grief of each person who sat in the back of the vehicle holding on to the flag as if they wanted to hold on to the person who was lying in the casket one last time. It was a very somber moment.

At the "four corners" of Disney, each vehicle made a right turn toward the flight line, where the members of the fallen soldiers' unit would say their last goodbye.

These caskets would then be loaded into a large aircraft and flown back to the United States to the fallen soldier's families.

I can't help but wonder if that was me in that casket. I would have never had the chance to tell my daughters how proud I am of them, how much I love them, and how I will always be there for them. I would never have had the chance to kiss Clinton one last time, to hold his hand. To look into his amazing and caring brown eyes and tell him how much he meant to me.

Clinton, I love you. I love you with all my soul. I am so proud of you. Proud of you as a father, a husband, and my best friend. No matter where life takes us, no matter what happens here, no matter how much time or distance separates us I will love you forever. I will always carry you in my heart. You have given me such a life I would never have known otherwise. I am a better person because of you.

34

— . —

AND THEN THERE WERE FOUR

"Bad news isn't wine. It doesn't improve with age."
- Colin Powell

A fghanistan, June 1, 2009

Today, this very day, four American soldiers died.

I'm sure when they started out their morning, each of these soldiers had no idea it would be their last day on earth. Their last day to see blue skies, the last day to feel the strong wind hit their face, the last day to talk to their children, wives, and other loved ones. Today was it for them.

Fate has a strange way of playing itself out. With one choice we make, we have no idea what or how that choice would potentially affect our lives. For the good or bad. Today, my young 20-year-old patient, whose birthday was just May 23, was supposed to be the primary driver on their mission. Being the driver was something he had done day in and day out. But today, today was different. As my patient began to enter the vehicle, one of the Sgt's stopped him and said jokingly, "I can't stand the way you drive. I'm doing the driving today," and just like that, fate happened.

My 20-year-old patient climbed in the back seat of the vehicle where the Sgt would usually sit, and off they went. As they were driving in the streets of a village just outside our base, the vehicle hit an IED, killing everyone except for two.

You see, my 20-year-old patient, who now lay flat on his back with an external fixator keeping his legs together in the TICU, was alive because he took the seat of the Sgt who, on a whim, decided to drive today. Sadly, the Sgt. was now one of the 4 who died in this IED blast.

This Sgt. had a wife and an infant daughter back home. As my patients Sgt. Major and Commander came to the bedside to deliver the news that he was only one of two sole survivors; he began to cry out for the Sgt. He was in shock.

He then asked to speak to his mother.

I quietly retrieved the phone and began to dial his mother's number. As I dialed, I remembered how I hated to make these calls. It never gets easier, no matter how many calls I have made since being here. It never gets easier.

It is difficult to know that you are the first person the family is going to hear from about their loved ones being injured in the line of duty.

This phone call was no different. The phone rang, and my patient's mother answered the phone cheerfully and then I said, "Hello, my name is Capt. Christine Collins. I'm calling from Bagram Air Base, Intensive Care Unit." The mother's silence was deafening. My very next words were, "Your son has been injured in the line of duty, but is doing well, and he would like to speak to you." The mother instinctively began to cry. I again reassured her that her son was okay.

It seemed like it took everything inside of her to keep it together. She spoke to her son for about 10 minutes, and before my patient hung up, he handed the phone to me. I was upset for his mother. As her voice shook and cracked as she said, "Does my son have both his legs?"

I said, "Yes of course, he has both his legs and arms, he is doing quite well and please know we are taking very good care of him."

I didn't realize until after we hung up that my voice was also shaky, and I had tears in my eyes. I wanted to cry for the mother who couldn't be with her son, who, I'm sure, was worried and scared for him. What the mother didn't know was how lucky her son was today. How fate took a turn and spared her son's life but took another life instead.

How does all of this make sense?

It's so chaotic and random.

One day, your buddy is with you, standing by your side, and the next day, he or she's dead.

Our night continued to be hectic and chaotic with more random trauma patients.

More sad stories.

More phone calls home.

Two more calls are made. To the wife of a 28-year-old soldier who is now a paraplegic and to another wife whose husband is in danger of losing both his legs. How can this ever get easier?

It won't, it can't, and it never will.

All we can do is remain steadfast and provide unconditional love and support to our fellow brothers and sisters in arms. To be here for eachother so that, together, we can get through these difficult days.

35

— • —

COMING TO AN END

"It is good to have an end to journey toward; but it is the journey
that matters, in the end."
—— Ursula K. Le Guin, American author

Afghanistan, June 17, 2009

When I look back over the 167 days that have passed, at
times, it seemed as if the time was at a standstill.

Now, standing where I'm standing, it seems like it was yesterday
when I said goodbye to Clinton and the girls so early in the morning
that the sun had not risen yet. When I close my eyes, I can vividly see
everyone and everything that unfolded on January 1st.

I remember wanting to go but not wanting to go.

I remember holding onto my girls and not wanting to let them go.

I remember holding onto Clinton and crying in his arms, thanking
him for being so strong and loving me so much.

I wasn't sure which path this journey would have taken me, but I
was willing to go where it would lead me.

Today, I'm here. Almost at the end of this magnificent journey,
this life-changing journey. Today was our "Re-deployment" ceremony.
This is where we received our NATO and Afghanistan medals. I also
received a third medal from the French. Each medal means something

different to me, and I am so honored to have been the recipient of each one.

When I look at each of these medals, I can see the faces of the many soldiers who have died. Their faces I will carry with me forever.

I can see their names and disfigured bodies, holding their hands, giving a part of myself to each of them, wiping the tears from their faces as they cry because they are the sole survivor of their convoy.

I can see my own face in these medals, wiping my own tears from my face for the loss of American troops or the lives we worked so hard to save and could not.

I can see the faces of the many loved ones who have been left behind by their fallen sons and daughters here in this country.

I can see the face of the French soldier, Trevor, who I will never forget and will forever remember what it took to save him.

I can see little Razia and her family, seeing her run to my arms and laugh.

I can see Begum, her smile that lights up a room, and her dancing in the hospital hallways with Olivia and me.

I can see little Jane with only one eye due to a gunshot wound to the head.

I can see the arm of my first American loss with his son and daughter's faces tattooed to his right forearm.

I can see Farah and the people of Farah, which I took care of.

When I look at each of these medals, I see so much. The memories of this place flood my mind and heart.

Today was a special day. A day for me and my fellow comrades to share and be proud of what we accomplished as a team. We did something great here. We changed, and saved lives. We facilitated everyday miracles.

*Capt Christine Collins, awarded the US Army Commendation Medal
for lifesaving actions for a fellow Army soldier*

36

— • —

A DOSE OF REALITY

"I held my breath and waited for the earth to stop spinning. The sun need not rise again. There was no reason for the rivers to flow. Birds would never sing."
— Laurie Halse Anderson, American author

Afghanistan, June 20, 2009

It was about 2 o'clock in the morning when my technician and I began to provide morning care to one of our critically ill patients.

As we talked about how busy we were there was a sudden loud boom that rocked the hospital. At first, we all stopped what we were doing and just looked at each other. Just like many times before, we would hear loud explosions and would continue working without skipping a beat.

This time was different.

The next thing I know, there is an operating room technician running into the TICU, yelling for blankets. I looked at her and saw that she was sobbing; I asked her, "What's the matter, what happened?" She said, "We were just bombed, and his head is missing!"

I ran as fast as I could to grab as many blankets as my arms could hold and my legs could carry. I went directly to the ER, and there rolled in an American soldier who was dead. He was killed in action during this rocket attack. His head was missing, and blood was everywhere.

The next American came rolling in. He was pale, clearly in shock, and his left leg was dangling by a small piece of skin.

The next thing I heard was my name being called, "Capt. Collins, we need you to take all the walking wounded in the ER bays!"

I left the trauma bay and began to see and treat the walking wounded that came through the doors. I called the TICU for more nurses. As one by one, wounded Americans came in, we quickly assessed their wounds, cleaned their cuts, started IVs, and got them the proper X-rays to confirm broken bones and appropriate treatment.

As things began to calm down, I needed to get back to the TICU. We were completely full and needed more backup. I already had three patients, two of whom were critically ill and unstable. I was not alone in this. The other 4 nurses who stood by my side today were in the same boat. Each of them had 3 critically ill patients.

Strangely enough, this, by far, was the longest and shortest day of my deployment.

I thought I was never going to end. For 14 hours, I didn't have time to sit, eat, or go to the bathroom. I was bouncing from one bed to the next. Then the traumas hit, and I didn't even have time to think. It was as if I had seen this so many times and had been so well-trained that my training just took over. It was instinct.

At the end of the two crazy hours, we lost 2 American soldiers and several wounded, with one losing his right leg.

It's amazing to me that the Taliban is getting better and better with the aim of their rockets. Each rocket is getting closer and closer to where we are. My time here can't end soon enough. We all live here day-by-day, thinking that "it" will never happen to us. The "it" is best described as getting bombed, losing a limb, or, even worse, losing our lives. But "it" happens. It's all around us, and it's scary.

This place puts things into perspective for me and for the others I serve with. We are all in this together. We can look into each other's eyes and know that we have gone through something that will forever bond us together. As my time draws down, I begin to reflect on where I came from, how I have changed, now what I see through these green eyes, and how I see things so differently.

Being here makes me appreciate the luxuries that await me at home, like driving my car down the street, talking on a telephone, being able to take a shower without wearing shower shoes, drinking clean water, not having to carry my 9mm Beretta sidearm and knife everywhere I go. Or better yet, feeling safe in my own home. Not being rocketed at night or hearing sirens or banging on our doors at night telling us we needed to report for 100% accountability with full body armor on and gas mask in place. Loving my children and husband. Trusting your neighbor or the person you work with, knowing they are not feeding information to the Taliban so that they have a chance to kill you. This is life. This is the reality here.

I have 13 days and a wake-up call before I begin my journey home.

I thank the heavens above for this dose of reality. We are at war and will continue until way after I leave this place. I thank God for putting things in perspective for me so that I can continue to serve my country, my fellow soldiers, and my family with honor.

37

SAYING GOODBYE IS NEVER EASY

"The two hardest things to say in life are hello for the first time and goodbye for the last."
— Moira Rogers, writer

A fghanistan, June 24, 2009

I had just finished a long 13-hour shift.

I was busy with a new admission. A 26-year-old Canadian had stepped on a pressure plate that triggered a mine/IED blast that blew his left leg completely off and severely damaged his left arm. This patient was completely unstable, and I was rapidly infusing ten units of cryo, fresh frozen plasma (FFP), packed red blood cells, bicarb, and bags of normal saline one after another. Not to mention all his other medications that needed to be given, labs, blood gases, dressing reinforcements, and doppler of the lower right leg and both arms.

My night flew by. As dawn broke, I saw Dr. Elwood, our pediatrician who has been the primary physician on little Razia's case. He stopped by to tell me that there was a slight possibility of Razia going home today. After the night I had and being completely exhausted, I remained long after my shift was over to find out more details as to when little Razia would potentially be discharged. As two hours passed, I could not get a clear answer whether or not she would be going home. So, I decided to go to my room and sleep to prepare for another night in the TICU.

Just as soon as my head hit the pillow, I was out like a light. My mind drifted to some far-off distant dream. I can still remember the sky was blue as the ocean, there were beautiful snow capped mountains, and I was running through a rolling hill of green grass. My dog Sadie was with me. We just made it to a large old oak tree, where we just sat. I can still smell her brown fur under my nose. Within an instant, I heard someone call my name.

At first, I thought it was in my dream, but as I slowly awoke, I could see someone peering into my small space behind the sheets that I'd placed around my bed to act like makeshift walls.

I recognized the voice. As I quickly came to my senses it was my boss, LTC Coddington. She was here to tell me that Razia was on her way home and that she wouldn't leave until she said goodbye to me. I immediately jumped out of bed and got dressed. I was still partly asleep as I opened the door to the outside. I was almost immediately blinded by the bright sun that hit my face. As I squinted and tried to make my way down the concrete stairs and across the road to the hospital entrance, all I could think to myself was, "Gosh, this is it. Razia is finally going home." I had a mix of emotions, and as I walked into her room, she just looked at me and began to smile.

I kneeled next to her bed and gave her the biggest hug. I began to cry. I couldn't believe that the time had finally come. The time for her to go home with her father and mother.

When I looked at her, I could vividly remember what she looked like when she first got here. She had made a huge transformation. One that most people thought couldn't or wouldn't happen. I began to think about all her "firsts."

Her first smile, first words to me, first hug, first wave, first steps, her first trip outside. Hearing her sing for the first time. Seeing her face light up when I gave her a cup of Pepsi. Seeing how she was calmed and soothed as I sang to her, holding her tightly as if I were her mother.

I thanked her father for being such a wonderful support system and for never giving up on his daughter. I told him that I would remember him and his family for the rest of my life, and I would always be here if they needed anything. I consider Razia my 4th daughter. My life will never be the same since meeting her and caring for her. She has touched so many people's lives here and abroad. I gave my good wishes to Razia and told her that I hope someday she can go to school and become a nurse or doctor to help her country and continue to make a difference and touch other lives as she has touched mine. I told her how smart she was that she could do anything she wanted to. The sky's the limit.

As we took one last stroll down the hospital corridors and one last walk through the TICU, we were out the front door—out for good this time. We were not going for a walk around the hospital. We were taking the walk to the van that would finally take her to her mother. The mother who has not seen her in almost 3 months. I can't help but wonder what life will be like for my little Razia.

Will she cry? Will she miss us? Will she be okay? Will she be loved by her family like she once was seconds before the bombing?

All these things run through my mind, and I have to tell myself that she will be loved, and she will be cared for and she will always know that I love her.

38

— . —

THE REPLACEMENTS

"Oh yes, the past can hurt. But you can either run from it, or learn from it."

- Rafiki

Afghanistan, July 4, 2009

As the days grow longer and longer with more injuries that enter our doors, both Olivia and I are waiting with wide-open eyes.

We are waiting for our replacements to come any day now. With each passing day we look for some type of relief, some type of hope that we would see a familiar face with each bus load of new personnel that arrive every night.

We prepared for another busy night. With a surge of new troops entering the eastern providences of Afghanistan, we knew the next few days would be the bloodiest days seen to date for not only the nationals, Afghan Army, and Police but most importantly for our American soldiers. Our love and compassion, which we had an overabundance of 6 months ago, now runs low. Our smiles are now dim. We are all looking for some relief. Every day before work, we tell each other that we can get through another day, we will not let this place get us down, and we remind ourselves that we have each other.

We will get through this.

As my night progressed, I worked like I had never worked before. I was assigned two sick Americans with respiratory failure who are both on ventilators to keep them alive. Both patients have a strange type of pneumonia, which has almost taken each of their lives. I worked diligently, and with every minute that went by, I began to titrate different pressor drips to keep their blood pressures at a particular level so that their major organs could perfuse and remain oxygenated. I then began to infuse multiple blood products on the second patient in bed 10; he was the worst of the two. After several hours, both patients began to stabilize, and now it was the "waiting" period.

Waiting to see how each patient would respond to the assortment of interventions that were completed and waiting for lab results.

As things begin to settle down, I hear an overhead page around the hospital that states that we have new arrivals waiting under the overhang by the ER. Unlike many nights before, I did not allow myself to get my hopes up, and neither did Olivia. Both Olivia and I gave a report to another nurse so that we could leave our patient's bedside for a moment. Olivia and I left the TICU with a deep-seated hope that we would find the one person who was sent to replace us.

We walked down the long corridor of the hospital and pushed back the double doors of the ER. We both stood there in disbelief. There were so many people scrambling around to find their bags. At first, the scene took me back to the first night that I arrived at the hospital over 180 days ago.

There was no rhyme or reason to any of this madness. I began to think that I was going to stay here forever, but as I made my way through the mass of people, I felt a small nudge on my right arm. At first, I thought it was someone who bumped into me, but there was the same nudge again. I looked to my right, and there he was...MY REPLACEMENT! All the way from Nellis Air Force Base, my replacement was finally here. My vision became blurry with tears because now I knew that I would finally be going home.

I could now see the light at the end of the tunnel. My attention was then moved to hearing Olivia's voice. I could hear the exhilaration in her voice; she was not too far from where I was standing. I could see her hugging and laughing with her replacement from Travis Air Force Base. Each of us held tight to our replacements and did not want to let them go. This moment was our saving grace.

The countdown began. We had two days to train both nurses. Both nurses were assigned dorm rooms and had 6 hours to rest and then be at work the next morning for in-processing. Their day on the 5th of July was long with briefings and signing off on their newcomer's checklist. Both replacements were sent home at 1500 to be back to work at 1900 hours to start a night shift.

My replacement's first night was cut short. Both Olivia and I trained in paperwork and computer charting. We went over how we get an admission, the diverse types of admissions, and the injuries we received. We gave them packets of paperwork to review in their rooms so that they would have the paperwork down and be rested and ready to work the next night. After 4 hours, we let our replacements go home to sleep and get prepared for the next night of work.

They are going to need all the sleep they can get.

Coming here and doing what we do is unforgiving and relentless when it comes to sleep and personal recovery. It was and still is NEVER about us. It is about the job we do 24 hours a day and how we do our job. We save lives, and those lives depend on us being here regardless of if we are "not ready" or "unprepared." For the sake of that one life we may save, we have to "be ready," and we must be "prepared."

It is a matter of life or death.

Over the next 12 hours was a roller coaster of training. Both nurses were ready and flexible to learn anything and everything. The night of the 5th into the 6th was the last day. Both Olivia and I worked throughout the night and finished at 0900. It was another 16-hour day for us; we both were tired; we were emotionally and physically drained. As we began to leave the hospital, we were notified that we would be leaving that night. We looked at each other in disbelief. We were going home.

At last, we were going home. Olivia and I started this journey together and we were finishing this journey together. This amazing expedition that would change both of us and one ride we would never forget.

39

— . —

MY LAST 72 HOURS

"Old things are replaced by new ones but the only old ones that can't be replaced are the ones with something with our lives."
—— Anthony Castillo

Afghanistan, July 10, 2009

Just ten hours after my last shift, I was waiting outside the building to process through customs at Bagram.

Olivia and I stood side by side like we've done so many times before, but this time, we were not saving anyone's life or slamming a large amount of blood products into someone's body who was bleeding out. We were beginning our journey home together.

We chose not to look back once we entered and passed through customs. We sat quietly and waited to be escorted to our C-17 aircraft that would fly us to Manas.

We had both been up for 2 days straight at this point. We were finally able to get comfortable on the broken benches we sat on.

Finally, at 0900 on July 7th, our group was notified that our plane was ready to board. We all wiped the sleep from our eyes and popped a stick of gum in our mouths to hide our morning breath. Excitement filled the air.

The C-17 was large, and our 35-member team looked so small sitting in such an enormous aircraft. The flight couldn't come fast enough. I had some time to reflect on the last 6 months and 2 weeks and all that I had seen and experienced. As we flew into Manas, I felt like a stranger. This world here was so much different than where I had come from. Everyone appeared to be laid back, with no care in the world. I could tell that I was tense and on edge. I was waiting to hear the sound of bombs, rockets, crying, and hurt soldiers.

But that wasn't coming. There was none of that here. It was just peaceful and quiet. I felt out of my element and still do.

As Olivia and I in-processed, we turned in our chemical warfare gear, body armor, and all the little extras that weighed us down by 50 lbs. It felt so good not to have that equipment anymore. By the time we were done with turning in our gear it was already 1700 hours. We were exhausted, so tired that we made our way to our tent, found a bunk bed, and fell fast asleep until midnight. It was an unrestful sleep filled with fast moving dreams and a quick wake-up with the uncertainty of where I was.

The rest of the morning was quiet and calm. We were waiting for word as to when our aircraft would be departing Manas. The times of our departure changed at least 3 times. It left us frustrated. By our second day at Manas, we were on "lockdown" by 1500 hours on the 9th. Once we passed through customs a second time and waited in a large room with 200 Romanian soldiers, there was a voice on the loudspeaker that asked for 25 volunteers to help with unloading pallets and loading baggage on the plane.

At first, I said, "no fucking way". I remember coming to Afghanistan and helping with building pallets and loading the aircraft and finding that there was no benefit but a lot of arduous work and all-over body bruising. But this time was different; the passenger terminal personnel had offered first-choice seating for those who would help load the plane. Olivia and I were out of our seats and in line to volunteer.

It was funny because Olivia was unsure but went with me anyway. I told her not to worry that it would be fun as I chuckled under my voice. Needless to say, for 3 and a half hours, we worked our tails off in 100-plus-degree weather. Loading 5 large palates of luggage (mostly Romania's military equipment), but the reward was so sweet. Olivia and I were able to sit first class all the way from Kyrgyzstan to Romania, then to Baltimore, Maryland. I've never been so comfortable on a plane before. It was well worth the bruising and sweat.

As we arrived 13 hours late to BWI, for the first time in over 6 months my cell phone worked. I quickly called Clinton and simply said, "Hi". We both started laughing. It was so wonderful to find out that Clinton's mom, sisters Melanie and Jilly, were at the airport to pick me up, even though my next plane left in 3 hours. I felt rescued when I first saw Clinton's family. I felt safe and at home. Once we got to the hotel, I was able to take a deep breath and cried for the first time. I mean, I really cried. I cried like I had been wanting to cry for 6 months and couldn't.

All my sadness, hurt, anger, and joy began to come out. Rita, Melanie, and Jilly were right there to hug me and remind me that I was home and that everything would be okay. Before I knew it, the time had slipped through my fingers, and it was time to go back to the airport. I was able to take a long, hot shower for the first time in over 6 months. I was able to get ready in a normal bathroom with fresh, clean towels, and for the first time in a long while, I didn't have to wear flip-flops while in the shower.

Life was good.

Once we said goodbye, I was on the last leg of a long journey home. I boarded a United plane destined for LAX and then from LAX to Las Vegas. It seemed like the longest flight of my life. Once we began our final descent into LAX, there was an overhead page in the cabin for a physician to come to the back of the aircraft. I quickly looked around and found that no one responded. It seemed all too fitting. I rose from my seat and found a 30-year-old female who appeared to be seizing. However, she didn't mimic all the signs or symptoms, but she did mimic the signs of a drug overdose.

Come to find out, she had taken a slew of over-the-counter med-ications mixed with prescription medication. From Dramamine to several different types of antidepressants and antipsychotics. I was able to render medical aid and kept her stable with the plane's automatic external defibrillator and nasal cannula and popped in an IV until we landed. I stayed by her side to ensure her airway remained patent and passed her care off to the paramedics, who boarded the aircraft and took her to the local hospital. The United crew was thankful, but all I could think about was getting home to see Clinton and my three girls.

As I switched flights at LAX, the time quickly flew by. It was a short flight, and I had the pleasure of sitting next to Mary Murphy, who is one of the judges from the "So You Think You Can Dance" TV show. We talked part of the way, and she asked me if she could meet my family and provide me with a "celebrity escort." We both just laughed.

As we rode down the escalators and waited for the first train to take us to the terminal, there he was. There was Clinton. For the first time in 6 long months, he was finally standing right in front of me. And can you believe I didn't recognize him at first? It was Mary who said to me, "he's standing right in front of you!" When I looked at him and hugged him, the moment was everything and more I'd hoped for. I just melted into his arms. I could hear Mary just laughing in the background and we all three caught the next train to the terminal.

Once we got off the train and took one more escalator, I could see Taylor, then Kennedy, and then Reagan. Everything else was a blur. All I can remember is pushing a lady who was standing in front of me to the side and seeing Kennedy and Taylor run to me. Kennedy had made these amazing "Welcome Home" signs, and I just held onto the girls and didn't let go.

Reagan wasn't sure; in fact, she didn't want to come to me. She just looked at me as if she kind of knew who I was, but she wasn't sure.

I prepared myself for Reagan not to remember who I was so that it would hurt as much. I knew everything would be okay, and it would take some time for Reagan to become familiar with me again.

But now, that's all I have. I have time... time to enjoy my kids, time to sleep, and time to heal.

After hugging my girls and wiping the tears away, my family was there to greet me. It was so wonderful to see and hug my Nana, mom, dad, Gigi, Kristy, and her husband Chad with their son Ayden. It was like a dream come true. All I wanted to do was get home and hold my children.

I was still in disbelief. I couldn't believe that I was actually home. I would catch myself double-checking or pinching myself to ensure that I was not dreaming. By the time I arrived at home, I was exhausted. I couldn't keep my eyes open. I tried my hardest to stay awake, but the fatigue got the best of me. As I lay in the comforts of my own home, in my own bed, safe and quiet, I began to reflect on my time in Afghanistan.

During my final days at Bagram, I've come to know myself better and in a different way. All that I've done had a purpose, whether I know or understand that purpose. I know the lives I've touched and the care I provided was the best I could have given. The people I met and grown to love; I will miss. The children I had cared for and the soldiers' hands I have held will be with me for an eternity. Those lives we work so hard to save, and couldn't I know I will see on the other side once it's my turn.

I may have physically left Afghanistan, but a part of me will always remain.

Collins and her dad, Clyde Elmer

40

— . —

COMING HOME

"Not until we are lost do we begin to understand ourselves."
– Henry David Thoreau

T uba City, Arizona

December 30, 2009

(*Five months after returning home*)

Coming home was not what I thought it would be. It has been a roller coaster of emotions and challenges that have lent themselves to me left and right.

Coming home to my family...I had waited for that day for well over 6 months. To hold my youngest daughter, hoping she would remember me. Looking into the eyes of my husband and feeling his strong arms wrapped around me was something I dreamt about for many days. To see my other two daughters with tears in their eyes, running to me as I stepped off the plane, yelling, "Mommy...mommy." Well, that day finally came and went. How I learned so much about myself and those that I care about. Some things have changed and will never be the same...the family I came home to is now different.

My husband is as solid as the deep-layered granite that lines the earth; my oldest daughter is wiser in the fact that she knows more about life and the realities life can bring. My middle daughter tells me every night how much she loves me and doesn't want me to go, and then there is my youngest...it's been 5 months since I've been back, and she has finally realized that "mommy" is no longer in Afghanistan when you ask her where I am...she is able to look at me and say, "Mommy's right here" and she is now able to tell me she "loves me."

It's been a challenging 5 months, and to the credit of my husband Clinton, who has been by my side without waiver and who has held me through the toughest of the days and nights. Telling me that I will be okay and that he loves me unconditionally, he has been MY saving grace through all of this. When I needed someone the most, he was there...he has always given me that "Free Pass." Meaning that no matter what I've done since my return, yelling, crying, breaking down at the most ridiculous things, letting me stay in my pajamas for days, supporting my choice in not wanting to go or do anything for the holidays...letting me just cry. He was there, all while others turned their backs on me and left me standing alone, alone in a world in which I was confused and lonely, even though I had my children and husband. I felt so alone inside.

It's so hard to explain; my coming home to the outsider looking in would appear to be "perfect," but in reality, it was far from perfect. At times, I would give anything to go back and do what I was doing in Afghanistan...there was so much meaning and purpose to my everyday events. Going to work in Bagram, I knew that I was doing something amazing...something that I knew was going to be life-changing. It's hard to look back and see it all gone, and at times, it feels like it was a dream or a blur. It's so hard to let it all go because I don't ever want to forget what the true meaning of sacrifice is and was. I feel, somehow, if I let it go, then that part of me that I gave so much of will be lost, and I won't be able to find it.

It's hard to live every day like a normal person, doing normal things, when in the back of my mind, I remember where I've come from and how it's changed my life and my family's lives. It's hard to be looked at as a "regular" person when thinking about Afghanistan, and what we did on an everyday basis was nothing short of extraordinary.

Nothing was regular in Afghanistan; there was no such thing as a "normal" day...living there for 6 months and 15 days was amazing. The funny thing about all of this, was I knew at the time, I was living an extraordinary life...every day of it. I just didn't know or realize the impact of living that way until now.

Over the past 5 months, there have been many changes that have developed. I've decided to leave the Air Force after 14 years of service...I have now entered a different realm of the military and have found a new home and family with the United States Public Health Service of the Commissioned Corps. Clinton, our three girls, and I packed up all our belongings and left Nellis Air Force Base for a new journey. We made the trip to our new home in less than 5 hours to Tuba City, Arizona. I decided to work with the underserved community of the Indian Health Service. It's been so healing to be here...this is a place where I can connect with myself...I can feel the soothing nature of the Navajo people and their land. Being here gives me great strength and solitude. I believe I needed this place and these people more than they needed me; however, my new boss would say differently.

My mornings are early, and my days are long, and in so many ways, this place reminds me of Afghanistan. We have interpreters that we use; I provide care for people without running water and electricity in their homes...much to everyone's surprise, these people live in "mud huts" known as Hogan's. The wonderful thing about being here is that my family is here with me to share in this experience and I am helping those in the United States of America who need it so desperately. In coming here, I received a promotion, and I'm able to make a greater impact on those patients and the staff that I lead.

However, the cries of the pediatric clinic right by my office constantly bring me back to my time in Afghanistan...hearing the cries of the children with lost limbs, burnt faces, and burnt bodies. The cries of the children from a war-torn country...every day, I think about all those children and the men and women I cared for.

I am lost...

41

— . —

THE CRIES OF A MOTHER

"A mother's grief is as timeless as her love."
— Joanne Cacciatore

Tuba City, Arizona, May 17, 2010

(10 months after returning home)

It was a regular Monday with a slight breeze in the air, enough to pick up the fine, rust-colored dirt that flew around in the sky in Tuba City so effortlessly. I remember walking outside in the late afternoon, closing my eyes, still feeling lost. I began to think about Carlo Robinson, who was the American soldier who died in January of last year.

Many times, in the quiet corners of my mind, Carlo comes to me through my thoughts and dreams. The pictures in my mind are vivid, painted with bright, brilliant colors, and my dreams still echo the picture of his two children tattooed on his right forearm.

When Carlo comes to me in my dreams, he never talks; he just points to certain pictures of where he came from. It's as if he's trying to tell me something. During these moments, I will sit quietly and recount the moments when I first met him and our team, which worked so diligently to save his life. No one wanted to give up, and by the end, there wasn't a dry eye in the room.

Everyone who was working on Carlo was in tears. It wasn't that we lost a person to our team. It was so much more than that. We knew that we had just lost a father. We lost someone's son, someone's grandson. We had just lost an American hero.

As I look around my surroundings, I can see my husband, my children, with our dogs. I think to myself how lucky I was to come home, and then I will gently bring up Carlo with Clinton and my experiences while in Afghanistan. Some days, my time overseas seems like a blur, and then other days, I'm talking myself out of the thought that I'm not in Afghanistan. Those brief moments of feeling as if I'm deployed lead me to the point in which I can't breathe or feel like I can't move a single muscle.

It seems as if, without even knowing it, my mind drifts away, and I can see, smell, and even taste moments of being deployed, yet I'm here in the safety of my own home or workspace.

There have been many days I've wanted to find Carlo's family. I wonder if they think about how he died, if they wonder if he was alone, or if he was in pain. In my dreams, I can see myself meeting his two children and telling them how wonderful their dad was. Last week I was able to make headway on where I could find Carlo's family, and today was the day I was going to make that call. I first tried his grandmother; it took me three times to actually dial the full number. Initially, the phone rang—and rang and rang with no answer. I had another number for Jennifer Robinson, but I wasn't sure who this Jennifer person was.

Was it his wife? His sister? Or possibly an Aunt?

I decided to dial the number to see where it takes me. A gentle, soft voice answered on the other side of the receiver, saying, "Jump'n Jacks." At first, I froze. I didn't know what to say or how to say who I was and what I wanted. It was like I had a million things to say all at once, but nothing would come out.

For the first time in a long time, I couldn't get a word out. The voice on the other side grew silent. I cleared my voice and said, "Hello, I'm looking for Ms. Jennifer Robinson," and the sweet voice on the other side said, "This is she," in a reluctant tone. I then said, "Uhm, I'm Captain Christine Collins, and I was in the Air Force stationed in Bagram....uhm... I'm calling about Carlo Robinson. Do you know him?"

The soft voice began to cry.

At this point, I still did not know who Jennifer was, but what I did know was that she knew Carlo. Everything inside of me began to come out. All the emotion of that January 17th, 2009, moment began to come out, and I began to cry, and I cried hard.

I stated I was one of the trauma critical care nurses who took care of Carlo, and I felt compelled to let his family know that we did everything we could to save his life. I wanted his children to know that he was a brave and wonderful man and that he did not die alone. I was with him the whole entire time, and I held his hand, stroked his face, telling him it was going to be okay".

I then asked, "Who are you?"

She said quietly and through her tears, "I'm Carlo's mother."

I told Ms. Robinson how sorry I was that he passed but that we held him for her and loved him for her, and he was not in any pain when he died. She began to cry. The sounds of her crying were almost too unbearable to hear.

It was as if you could hear her soul tearing and ripping apart. You could hear the emptiness in her voice and the loss in her breath.

The loss of her baby had rocked her to the core. She said, through her tears, "God has answered my prayers, and I've always wondered if he was alone. I wondered if he was cold or if he was in pain. I've had so many questions but no one to answer them." Carlos' mother began to cry out, "My son, my baby, my baby...he's gone!"

I felt as if I couldn't breathe. It was hard to swallow or even speak as I stood fast, listening to Carlo's mother's gut-wrenching cries and moans. Her soul, her heart, was broken. Her life has forever been changed.

As we continued to talk, my good friend Kristy Scherbring was at my side. Without fail, she has been there from the day I returned. With all the ups and downs, the anger, the rages, the moments where I felt like dying because the grief was too much to bear. Kristy sat next to me as Carlo's mother cried, and I cried.

As I finished my conversation with Jennifer, I made a promise to come see her and meet Carlo's family and that I would always be here for her, no matter what time or day. I would only be a phone call away. Jennifer's soft and quiet voice thanked me, and I could tell that something had changed by the end of our conversation, as if there was a newfound resilience in her voice. We both are mothers in different stages of our lives, but we are mothers who love their children and have found a bond in the most unlikely situations.

I feel a connection with Carlo's family. I'm not sure where it will take me, why it's so strong, or why Carlo. After all, there were so many other soldiers I took care of. But this is what it is, and I recognize the fact that somewhere, somehow, I will need to be of service to this family. For Carlo's children who will grow up without a father. For a mother who lost a good son too soon. For Carlo, who is looking down upon me right now, knowing I will do right by him, even though we only met briefly, and that moment has been etched in my soul to where I will carry a small piece of him wherever I go.

42

---·---

SGT CARLO M. ROBINSON

"Rest and be thankful."
—— **William Wordsworth**

F ebruary 1, 2013
   (4 years after returning home)

"There Are Still Caring People in the World"

On my return flight from Chicago this weekend, I read a touching story in Ladies Home Journal *about an Air Force nurse who later reconnects with the family of an Army sergeant who she nursed as he was dying. There I was, sitting at my gate, with waterfall tears, not because of my canceled flight, but because of this bittersweet story. As a mother of three young children, I cannot even imagine the grief our military families must endure upon the news of such tragedies. Although this story involves the loss of an innocent young man's life, it also illustrates, as his mother, Jennifer, states, "It's good to know that there are still such caring people in the world." I wanted to share this inspirational story. – Claire Patterson, blogger.*

From Ladies Home Journal, 2013

"I Finally Met the Woman Who Held My Dying Son"

When Jennifer Robinson's son was killed in Afghanistan, she thought she'd never know the details of his last moments -- until a phone call from Air Force nurse Christine Collins changed everything.

As told to Jessica Brown

A Day that Changed Everything

On January 17, 2009, a roadside bomb hit an Army vehicle near the U.S. military base in Kabul, Afghanistan. This tragic event changed -- and ultimately united -- the lives of two women: Captain Christine Collins, an Air Force nurse on duty at a hospital near Kabul, and Jennifer Robinson, whose son was an Army staff sergeant stationed nearby. This is the amazing story of how their paths intersected and how two mothers helped each other heal.

Christine Collins: When we learned that six of the soldiers wounded in the blast were on the way to our ICU, the staff put together a plan in a matter of seconds. I was assigned to be the medication nurse for the second patient who arrived, a 33-year-old male. In an emergency, you learn little about your patient beyond the most basic facts. I didn't even know the soldier's name. I did know, however, that he was a father. When I saw him, my eyes went immediately to the faces of two children tattooed on his right arm. I thought of my three daughters back home in the States, whom I missed desperately. We must save this man, I thought. His children need him. He was in bad shape, though. He'd lost a lot of blood, and his heart was barely beating. We gave him round after round of epinephrine and took turns doing chest compressions to try to get his heart pumping again. When that didn't work, the surgeon opened the soldier's chest and pumped his heart with his hands while we began transfusions of red blood cells and plasma. We worked for at least an hour. No one wanted to give up, but we couldn't save him. I took a moment to hold the soldier's hand, stroke his face, and tell him that everything would be okay. It was my duty as a mother to love him and comfort him in the last seconds of his life. By the time the doctor called the code, all of us were in tears.

It wasn't just that we lost someone on our side. We'd lost a father, a son, an American hero. I composed myself and gently washed his body so his fellow soldiers could come into the ICU to say goodbye. They would be the ones to tell me the man's name: Carlo Robinson.

Jennifer Robinson: Two men in uniform came to my doorstep in Hope, Arkansas, to inform me that Carlo had been killed. I couldn't believe it. We'd just spoken on the phone the day before! He was scheduled to go on leave in just a few weeks, and he was going to spend that time with me and his children, Carneshia and Dakaria. They were living with me while Carlo was serving overseas. All I'd been thinking was, I just want him to come home so I can see him. That's what I kept screaming when the soldiers gave me the news. I never thought Carlo would grow up to be a soldier. Some parents see it in their kids right away -- all the children talk about are their G.I. Joe toys. But Carlo wasn't like that. So, when he told me 14 years ago that he was joining the Army, I hadn't seen it coming. His decision to enlist didn't worry me -- 9/11 hadn't happened yet. We weren't at war. But in 2008, when Carlo was sent to Afghanistan, I got nervous. It was his first deployment, and he could have avoided it. He'd left the Army several months earlier, but he had trouble finding a job he liked, so he decided to reenlist. I think the military was part of him at that point. As scared as I was, I also felt proud of him for not settling for a job he wasn't meant to do and choosing to fight for freedom instead. The soldiers had few details about how Carlo died, just that a bomb had detonated near his vehicle. I was left with so many questions. Did he make it to the hospital? If so, did the doctors do everything they could to save him?

I prayed that the answers would come.

Healing Together

Five months after Carlo was killed, Collins's deployment ended, and she returned to the States. The transition to the life she'd had to leave behind was difficult, as it is for so many service members. Though Collins had been able to video-chat with her family while she was overseas, her youngest daughter, Reagan, 2, wasn't sure who Collins was at first. The family would gradually heal, but Collins felt like her work in Afghanistan wasn't done.

Christine Collins: I thought about Carlo a lot. When I looked back on that day, the images of him were so vivid. I could see the tattoos of his children on his arm.

And I wondered: What was his family going through? Did they worry about how he died, if he was alone or in pain? I'd remember the promise I made to my family before I went to Afghanistan: that I would give 110 percent of myself to everyone cared for there. If I was going to be away from them for a year, I had to make that time as meaningful as possible. It was, but there was more I needed to do. I had to find some sense of closure. I had to find Carlo's family. I found the name of the town he lived in online, so I did a little more digging and came up with the phone number for a Jennifer Robinson. Was she his wife? Maybe a sister? I had no idea. When Jennifer answered the phone, I froze. I didn't know how to say who I was and why I was calling. Finally, I found my voice. "I'm Captain Christine Collins, and I was in the Air Force stationed in Kabul," I said. "I'm calling about Carlo Robinson. Do you know him?" Jennifer began to cry, and soon I was crying, too. All the emotions of that day when I'd tried so desperately to save Carlo came tumbling out.

"I was one of the nurses who took care of Carlo," I explained. "I wanted to let your family know that we did everything we could to save his life. I wanted his children to know that he was a brave man and that he did not die alone. I was with him the whole time. I held his hand and stroked his face. I told him it was going to be okay." I took a breath and then asked, "Who are you to Carlo?"

Jennifer Robinson: "I'm his mother," I said. I almost couldn't believe what was happening. When Carlo was flown back to the U.S., there was a mix-up at the airport, and the wrong body was sent to the funeral home. It was a painful experience that made me question what's true and what isn't. But when Christine described Carlo's tattoo, I knew this was real. God had answered my prayers. I couldn't be with Carlo when he died, so God chose Christine to comfort him. Her team did everything they could to keep him alive.

Christine Collins: We talked for a long time that day. We're both mothers in different stages of our lives, but we are mothers who love our children. We formed a bond in the most unlikely situation. I told Jennifer that I would always be there for her no matter what. I wasn't physically close to her (I'm in Virginia), but I assured her I was only a phone call away. And one day, I said I would meet her and Carlo's children.

A Special Meeting

When Ladies' Home Journal *learned about all that Collins had done for Carlo's family, we knew we had to arrange for them to meet in person. Last May (2012)-- on Memorial Day weekend, appropriately -- LHJ flew Collins to Robinson's home in Arkansas.*

Jennifer Robinson: When Christine arrived, we hugged so hard and started crying immediately. I was holding the person who had held my son! I couldn't believe she'd gone so far beyond her duty to meet Carneshia, Dakaria, and me. Christine told me that in her dreams, she'd envisioned herself meeting the children and telling them how brave Carlo was. That day, I watched her do it. Her visit was bittersweet, though. Bitter because it opened old wounds; sweet because I was able to embrace the woman who was with Carlo when he died.

You don't meet people like Christine every day. It's good to know that there are still such caring people in the world.

Christine Collins: I learned so much about Carlo that day. Jennifer told me that the kids in Afghanistan always looked for him because he gave them candy when he was out on patrol. People nicknamed him "The Dentist" because he could make anyone smile. As we looked at photos of Carlo, I saw why it fit. His own smile was beautiful. I'm not sure why I feel such a strong connection to Carlo. But it's there, and I know I need to be of service to Carlo's kids, who will grow up without a dad, and to his mother, who lost her son. And I need to do it for Carlo, who's looking down on me, knowing I will do right by him even though we only met briefly.

Wherever I go, he'll always be with me.

43

— • —

Unzip With a Purpose

"By throwing yourself into these emotions, by allowing yourself to dive in, all the way, over your head even, you experience them fully and completely."

– Mitch Albom

To say or type the word, 'unzip', with zero context, something comes to mind for you.

I don't know what that is or might be, but I bet it's different for each of us. What if I tell you that for me to sit here and write, I need to be unzipped. Perhaps your thoughts shift again? Now if I add one more layer of context, perhaps a post-it note I wrote about what 'un-zipped' means, then we can move on with the story. Ok?

My post it note says this:

"Unzipped version. Raw motion, harsh emotion. Terror. Being afraid. Get the fuck off my mom."

That's it.

Fifteen words.

Those are the words on a post it note I keep on my computer screen as I write. Suddenly, with more context, I bet now when I say 'unzipped' it means something dramatically different. Maybe even nothing at all.

Would you like to know why I have that post-it note written and why I'm staring at it right now? Because what I really want this book to be is the complete, unzipped version of who I am.

Of what I've experienced.

Of whom I became.

Of whom I'm *still* becoming.

I am so used to being that armored-up person in life. That 'throat punch' Collins who is the tough one. The trauma nurse who strives not to cry in front of the troops. The mom who wants her daughters to be tough, self-sufficient, and not have to rely on anyone to have and to live the life they dream. After all, that's the person in my life story that I am and have become.

What I'm striving to do now is to be and show the unzipped, raw emotion, real version of myself. It's a part that people rarely, if ever, see, let alone read about.

As I sit at my desk, and before I start writing, I begin to gain a deep focus and draw from that little Post-it note. In fact, I meditate for a bit so that when the thoughts flow from heart to fingers to keyboard, it is as deep as I can let the words be. For me, it's been terrifying.

Back in 2009, I had things to do, people to treat, lives to save and that was my way of proving myself day in and day out. But today, right this moment, it's this book.

This book is how I want to prove myself. But not to the world, only to me.

So, I find myself staring at this post-it note on my computer screen. I feel the weight of those words settling into my bones. 'Unzipped version. Raw emotion, harsh emotion. Terror. Being afraid.' It's a reminder, a touchstone, a promise to myself to show up on these pages as I am and NOT as I think I should be.

It's a vulnerability that feels foreign to me, after so many years of armoring up, of being the tough one, the strong one, the one who never gives up. It's a role I've played so well, in so many aspects of my life – as a trauma nurse, as a protector, as a mother. And it's a role that has served me well, that has allowed me to survive and even thrive in the face of unimaginable challenges.

But there's a cost to that armor, to that unrelenting toughness. It's a weight that we carry, a barrier that keeps us from fully connecting with ourselves and with others. And as I've learned, both in the province of Farah and in the quiet moments of introspection, there is a strength in vulnerability, a power in allowing ourselves to be seen, really seen, in all our messy, imperfect humanity.

So, while I strive to unzip and release, I realize it's a process that is painful at times and brings up memories and emotions I've long kept buried. But it's also a process that is deeply healing, that allows me to reclaim my story and my sense of self in a way I never have before.

And I think, in a way, that's the journey we are all on.

The journey to prove ourselves, not to the outside world, but to the quiet voice within that knows our deepest fears and our highest hopes. The journey to embrace our vulnerability, our humanity, our inherent worthiness, even in a world that so often tells us we're not enough.

For me, my journey has so far taken the form of grueling training exercises and harrowing deployments, of long nights in the ICU and longer nights of the soul. It's taken the form of this book, of the words I'm pouring onto these pages, one raw, unfiltered truth at a time.

For you, it may look completely different. It may be in the quiet moments of self-reflection, in the brave conversations with loved ones, in the small, daily acts of courage that no one else sees. But no matter what form it takes, know this: your journey is valid, your story is worth telling, and your struggle and your strength are a testament to the resilience of the human spirit.

Keep peeling back those layers.

Keep unzipping that armor, one raw and honest truth at a time.

Keep fighting. Keep showing up. Keep being your messy, imperfect, beautiful human self.

44

— · —

THE WASHINGTON POST, 'IT HAS TO MEAN SOMETHING'

S eptember 5, 2021

(12 years after returning home)

A trauma nurse saved Afghans from the horrors of war. Now, she questions what their future holds.

Former Air Force Capt. Christine Collins, a trauma and critical-care nurse, is intimately familiar with the anatomy of war.

She knows, for example, that a human body can appear perfectly fine when observed from the front, even when the back of the person's head is entirely missing from a bomb blast set up by Taliban fighters. The same fighters bombing convoys would end up under her care, spitting and kicking in her direction as she treated them, too.

She also knows that any language barrier between injured Afghans and the American doctors holding their hands evaporated in moments of pain. She understands that a smile or a simple thumbs-up has the power to serve as a signal of love and hope in times of turmoil.

For her and many other medics, Collins said from her home in D.C., "it is an everyday struggle still."

When Collins left for Afghanistan in January 2009, the youngest of her three daughters, Reagan, was just 13 months old. "She was so tiny,"

Collins recalled. "A baby." During her time away from her family, she missed birthdays, anniversaries, and other milestones. Reagan's first tooth. The excitement of her first steps.

"I still have such guilt that I deal with over that," Collins said. The regret only fueled her to perform to the best of her ability in Afghanistan, she said. "I remember telling myself that if I'm going to be away from my husband and three children, it has to mean something."

Collins vividly remembers taking care of an Afghan teenager who had been raped and become pregnant. Her brother later admitted to taking her to a cattle shed to remove the fetus with a razor before sewing her back up with thick yarn. The 14-year-old's mother was also accused. After the forced abortion, the teenager, who was around five months pregnant, suffered a dangerous infection that almost killed her. "We took care of her from the time that she almost died with sepsis to the time she walked out," Collins said.

Now, the fate of that girl, whose dressing Collins changed hourly for weeks — and the fate of so many other Afghan nationals saved during the war — is again uncertain. Watching the news from Afghanistan, a place full of people she knows so well, has been "brutal," said Collins, who is now a captain in the Commissioned Corps of the U.S. Public Health Service.

Since mid-August, she has wrestled with frequent panic attacks. Her husband, Clinton, recites facts about hummingbirds to her in a bid to calm her down. It's like when he used to crawl into the closet alongside her after she returned from deployment when she was seeking a safe hiding spot away from the rest of the world.

For Collins, the level of sacrifice made in Afghanistan is hard to put into words. "You can't even put a price on that," she said. "We were ordinary people doing extraordinary things."

— Jennifer Hassan.

When the fall of Afghanistan happened in August of 2021, it was a dark period for me.

When the events became an international shitshow, and I learned of the devastating loss of thirteen of our troops, I felt that weight threatened to crush me entirely. The despair, the anguish, the overwhelming sense of hopelessness – it was like a tidal wave pulling me under.

Memories came flooding to mind, holding that tiny, broken child in my arms all those years ago; I felt the weight of all the pain and trauma that war leaves in its wake. The shattered lives, the shattered dreams, the shattered sense of hope for a better future.

In those dark moments, I sat with a knife, contemplating the unthinkable, ending my life.

I wanted to die.

I thought of my daughters, my husband, and the irreparable damage my actions would cause – it all seemed hopeless. I was ready to receive the darkness. In a way, he was smiling, beckoning, as the grim reaper made his way toward me. After all, death was an old friend of mine.

Since I already felt dead inside. I was simply going to make sure the outside matched the inside. Feeling so disconnected from the blessings in my life was a strange and awful feeling. I woke up every day and would go through the motions, putting a fake smile on and functioning and doing what needed to be done while carrying this dark secret, this unrelenting desire to not exist anymore.

People only see the beginning and the end of the war—the deployment scenes, the stuff the news shows, and then the homecomings. But what about afterward? When the dust settles? People like me come home with all our limbs attached. The injuries are invisible, but we know they are there.

We suffer in silence, and that's what fucking sucks. It's this piece of the war that's not seen. To the outside world I'm a retired veteran, mom, and wife. But inside?

I was screaming for help. I needed something.

What **I** actually **needed** was **SOMEONE**.

LTC Elizabeth "Liz" Coddington.

Liz was my commanding officer in Afghanistan. She always knew how to make things better, how to get supplies when we were low, and how to show up with lemon cake when there was no cake for miles in a tent in the middle of the desert.

She just knew.

When Olivia and I were in the thick of the everyday shit at Bagram, Liz was there. She never faltered; she was right next to us, shoulder to shoulder. We loved and respected the hell out of this woman. Immediately, Clinton said, "I'm buying you a ticket right now. There's no way that I can lose you, and there's no way that the girls can lose their mom. If it's this important to you and this is going to make a difference for you, I will buy you ten tickets."

I flew to Florida and was embraced by Liz. We talked, we spent time on the beach, and we talked some more. Liz was who I needed, and still, after all these years, she was right by my side. Liz doesn't know this, but that's the second time she's saved my life.

No matter how badly I wanted to end my life, the truth is, I would never do it. My kids would be devastated. And Clinton would be changed for life. I'm certain that they are the reasons that I can't and will not carry it out.

But the fact remains that I sometimes don't want to live, and that must be okay.

You see, going back through these raw emotions is hard.

It's like I got displaced back 15 years ago, and it's rehashing out all this shit. I've been through years and years and years of counseling, medication management, and psychiatrists and psychologists. When I step out of myself, well, I know it's helping because I would have been dead a long time ago.

Giving a voice to these thoughts and memories that I've kept locked away for so long is important. I know I'm not alone in this struggle. I know that so many of you reading this have faced your own battles with depression, PTSD, and the kind of soul-deep weariness that makes even the simple act of living feel like an unbearable burden.

And I want you to know that I see you, I hear you, and I understand the courage it takes to keep breathing, to keep putting one foot in front of the other, when every fiber of your being is screaming for release, for silence.

Your life, your story, your unique presence in this world – it all matters more than you can possibly imagine. Even on the darkest days, when you feel like nothing more than a placeholder, a shell going through the empty motions of existence – you are making a difference simply by being here. And I'm not bullshitting you.

You may not see it now. I know I struggle to see it in my own life, to find that sense of purpose and meaning that came so clear in the heat of battle, in the intensity of saving lives and serving something greater than myself. But I must believe that it's still there, waiting to be uncovered.

Maybe it's in the love you give to your family, the way you show up for them even when you feel like you have nothing left to give. Maybe it's in the work you do, the way you pour your heart and skills into making the world a little bit better, a little bit brighter. Maybe it's in the simple acts of kindness and compassion you offer to others, never knowing just how much those moments may mean to someone who is struggling just as much as you are.

Or maybe, just maybe, it's in the bravery of facing another day, of choosing to keep fighting even when every part of you wants to give up. Maybe that is a purpose powerful enough to keep you going.

I won't pretend it's easy. I won't offer you a quick fix or promise that everything will be okay. Because the truth is, some days it's not okay. Some days, it feels like it will never be okay again.

But on those days, I urge you to reach out.

To lean on the people who love you, who see your worth even when you can't see it yourself.

To seek help from professionals who understand the complexities of trauma and depression, who can offer guidance and support you on this fucked journey we call life.

And on the days when even that feels impossible, I want you to remember this: you are not a burden. You are not weak. You are not alone.

You are a warrior, a survivor, a bright and shining light in a world that needs you more than you know.

So, keep breathing, keep fighting, and keep holding on to the hope that tomorrow may bring a little more clarity, a little more ease, and a little more joy.

Trust that even on the hardest days, you are exactly where you need to be.

It was **Liz** that gave me the strength to keep going.

One breath at a time.

One step at a time.

One day at a time.

One small, brave act of living at a time.

Keep holding on.

Keep fighting.

Keep moving **FORWARD**.

45

SPACE AND GRACE

"Dying in war, well, it's not the worst thing that can happen."
- Christine Collins

R ockville, Maryland, January 2024
(15 years after returning home)

"Space and Grace" — Those three words and all that they mean keep me moving forward.

They are a reminder to allow myself the compassion and space needed to grow, and to heal, especially during those times where I don't feel worthy or good enough. These words are a reminder that there is a reason I'm here, even if I struggle at times to find and to see it.

Over the many years that have passed, I have come to realize that I've been lost, of course, not in the physical sense, but emotionally and mentally. I've been struggling with the loss of the person I once was — the Christine who left for war and never returned.

Through years of therapy sessions, I finally realized the painful truth: a part of me was lost in the fray, a piece that's unrecoverable.

Despite maintaining a facade of control, internally, I was unraveling, unable to understand my own thoughts and emotions.

The anger that stayed for years, the sudden waves of sadness, the loneliness that consumed me even when I had my loving family surrounding me — all pointed to a profound loss I couldn't explain. Reflecting on my homecoming, I recall the inquiries about my next "novella" — not literary fiction, but my unvarnished journals sent to Clinton, which found their way to a supportive readership.

These readers unknowingly became my pillars, offering unconditional love and support. Upon my return, they sought my voice and my presence, but I wasn't ready to discuss the raw truths of my experiences—the realities of war...survival, and death.

Back in the States, I doubted their ability to grasp the full extent of my ordeal. How could they, from the comfort of their homes, understand the journals that chronicled the traumatic realities of war? These weren't scripted performances; they were genuine narratives of sacrifice and loss. And though they wished for me to share these stories with their communities, I was entangled by bitterness, anger, and cynicism.

Looking back, I have some regret for not fulfilling their wishes, yet I recognize it wasn't their fault. They reached out with distant affection, which I wasn't prepared to share.

Perhaps, had I spoken out then, it might have helped my healing.

It's funny how time works. There are no redos and no going back; time is a one-way street.

So, with "Space and Grace" as my words, I continue to learn and will keep moving forward, no matter how tiny or massive each step may be.

46

—·—

RESILIENCE

"Resilient people possess remarkable optimism, mental agility, and awareness of self and surroundings. Strong emotional
intelligence and the ability to remain connected with others.
Choosing the resilient path is never an easy path. It can be a
lonely path."

--Christine R. Elmer Collins

That quote kept me around then.

And it keeps me around now.

Contemplating the path of resilience, the choice to keep going
even when the road is dark and the burdens heavy, I'm struck by the
parallels between my current life's journey and the one I walked in
Afghanistan.

The decision to see humanity, to choose compassion, even in the
face of cruelty and conflict. The willingness to venture into the unknown, to risk safety and comfort in the name of a higher calling.
And the quiet, unshakeable conviction that despite all the pain and
the struggle, there is still meaning to be found, still a reason to keep
putting one foot in front of the other.

I know many of you share this conviction, even if your battles look
different from mine. Because the truth is, we all face moments that

test our resolve, our faith, and our very sense of purpose. These are moments when the darkness feels overwhelming, and the path ahead seems impossible to navigate.

In those moments, it's tempting to give in to despair, to take off the rose-colored glasses and let the harsh, unfiltered reality of the world crush our spirits. But as I've learned, both in the hospital wards of Afghanistan and in the quiet hours of my own soul-searching, it's in those very moments that we must hold fast to our humanity—to our capacity for hope, compassion and finding light in the darkness.

That doesn't mean denying the reality of the pain or the hardship. It doesn't mean pretending that everything is okay when it clearly is not. Rather, it means making a choice—a choice to look for the good, even amidst the bad. to extend kindness, even when we're met with hostility. to believe in the possibility of change, even when all evidence points to the contrary.

It's a choice that is never easy.

As I wrote in my note to myself, the path of resilience can be a lonely one. It requires a level of mental and emotional agility that can be exhausting to sustain. But I truly believe it's a path worth walking. Because in choosing to be resilient, we not only save ourselves – we become a light for others.

When we show compassion to an enemy, we send ripples of humanity across the battlefield. When we venture into the unknown to help those in need, we inspire others to be brave. And when we share our stories of struggle and survival, we give hope to those who are still in the thick of their own battles.

That's the power of resilience. It's not just about bouncing back from adversity – it's about transforming adversity into a catalyst for growth, for connection, for positive change.

Recalling and remembering the fury and frustration I felt during many days in Afghanistan, caring for patients who seemed hell-bent on making my job as difficult as possible, I can't help but reflect on the larger lessons of that experience.

The reality is that life has a way of throwing us curveballs. Yes, especially the human, enemy combatant type, and of putting obstacles in our path that test our patience, our resolve, and our very sense of purpose. In those moments, it's easy to get lost in the anger, to let the negativity consume us. It's tempting to lash out, to give in to the desire to fight fire with fire. But as I learned that day, and in so many other moments throughout my journey, the true test of our character lies in how we choose to respond to adversity.

It's not about being perfect, or never feeling frustrated or angry. It's about recognizing those emotions for what they are – valid, human responses to challenging situations – and then making a conscious choice to rise above them. To stay focused on our higher purpose, even when every fiber of our being wants to give in to the chaos.

For me, that higher purpose was always about making a difference. Whether I was caring for enemy combatants in the hospital or facing down unruly individuals as a Security Forces troop, my goal was to be a force for good in the world. To stand up for what's right, even when it's hard. Even when it's scary as fuck.

Let's face it – you and I both know life is full of "throat punch" moments.

Moments when we're faced with a choice: to back down, or to stand our ground. To let fear and anger dictate our actions, or to rise above and stay true to our values. It's not an easy choice. It requires a level of courage and self-awareness that can be hard to muster, especially in the heat of the moment.

So, the next time you find yourself in a "throat punch" moment – and trust me, those moments will come – remember this: you have the power to choose your response. You have the strength to stay focused on your higher purpose, even when every instinct is telling you to lash out or give up. Embrace the anger, the frustration, the fear – and then let them go.

Breathe deep, stand tall, and remember who the fuck you are at your core. And then take that next step forward, with courage and compassion.

Every single one of us is fighting a battle of some kind. Every single one of us knows what it means to be broken, to be lost, to question everything we thought we knew. And yet, here we are. Still standing, still breathing, still finding the courage to keep going.

That, to me, is the true miracle of the human experience. Not that we live lives free from pain, but that we find ways to grow through it. That we learn to carry the weight of our scars, to honor the memory of those we've lost, and still find room for hope, for laughter, for love.

Reminding us that even in the darkest of times, there is still light to be found. That even when we are pushed to the brink of our endurance, there is still hope, still beauty, still the incredible resilience of the human spirit.

It won't be easy. But with the courage to speak our truth, to share our stories, to reach out and ask for the help we so desperately need, you will be heard. It starts with the willingness to see beyond the surface to acknowledge the invisible scars and the silent struggles that so many of us carry.

Together, we can support one another, to where we no longer suffer in silence, where the invisible scars are met with love and understanding instead of judgment and isolation. Continue to remain open to what the world has to offer and embrace each day.

Together, we will find our way home.

47

—·—

ABOUT THE AUTHOR

C hristine Collins left the Air Force in December 2009 and was commissioned in the United States Public Health Service, Commissioned Corps, retiring as a Captain in 2021 after 27 years of service. She remains a skilled trauma nurse and a resilient woman and writer.

Her experiences on the frontlines of war have shaped her life profoundly, leading her on a journey of healing, self-discovery, and unwavering commitment to helping others. Christine's memoir, *Service, Honor & Sacrifice*, is a raw and honest account of her time in Afghanistan and the battles she faced upon returning home.

As a mother of three daughters, Christine has fought hard to reconcile the harrowing realities of war with the love and light of family life. Her story is one of finding hope in the darkest of places and the transformative power of compassion.

Christine's story has been featured in Ladies' Home Journal and The Washington Post. She has been recognized for her service and her dedication to raising awareness about the unique challenges faced by veterans and their families.

When she's not writing or speaking about her experiences, Christine can be found spending time with her husband, Clinton, their daughters, and Michon. She remains committed to supporting and uplifting fellow veterans and to shining a light on the unsung heroes of the military medical community.

48

— . —

THE END

Christine Collins is a decorated veteran, having served as a U.S. Air Force Captain and trauma nurse during a pivotal deployment to Afghanistan in 2009. Stationed at Bagram Air Base, she found herself at the epicenter of the conflict, tirelessly working to save the lives of American troops, Afghan civilians caught in the crossfire, and even enemy fighters.

Through her raw and poignant memoir, Christine unveils the physical and emotional toll of war, not just on those fighting but also on the medical personnel tasked with picking up the pieces. Her vivid accounts transport readers to the heart of the conflict, revealing both the horrors and the glimmers of hope that sustained her. After returning to the U.S., Christine grappled with the invisible wounds of war, finding solace in writing as a means to process her experiences and to shed light on the often overlooked challenges faced by veterans.

As a wife and mother of three daughters, Christine's journey of healing and self-discovery is a testament to the resilience of the human spirit. By sharing her story, she hopes to foster a deeper understanding of the sacrifices made by our service members and to inspire others to find strength in the face of adversity.

Learn More
www.CombatCareWarrior.com

ISBN 979-8-9896594-1-8

Made in the USA
Las Vegas, NV
13 December 2024

14197453R00134